CONTENTS

This book is published as part of the celebration of *Céad Bliain Sinn Féin*, the hundredth anniversary of our party. It is dedicated to all Sinn Féin members and supporters.

Beirigí bua

GERRY ADAMS

THE NEW IRELAND

A VISION FOR THE FUTURE

A Brandon original paperback

First published in 2005 by Brandon
an imprint of Mount Eagle Publications
Dingle, Co. Kerry, Ireland and
Unit 3, Olympia Trading Estate, Coburg Road,
London N22 6TZ, England

2 4 6 8 10 9 7 5 3 1

ISBN 0 86322 344 3

Cover design by Anú Design
Cover photo by Liam Sweeney
Typesetting by Red Barn Publishing, Skeagh, Skibbereen
Printed in the UK

REAMHRA

The year 2005 marks the centenary of Sinn Féin. It is also the year, and this is a coincidence, that the IRA called an end to its armed campaign. The import of this momentous decision is still being absorbed at the time of writing by republicans and others. But undoubtedly it has opened up huge challenges and opportunities for all of us in the time ahead.

This short book is written in an attempt to sketch out a sense of modern Irish republicanism now and for the future. It is not a party political manifesto, more a personal statement, though obviously the bulk of my remarks here reflect Sinn Féin policy. Over the past century, Sinn Féin has been an idea, a name, a federation of political societies, a national independence movement, a republican campaigning organisation and, in 2005, the only all-Ireland political party and the fastest growing party in the country.

The words Sinn Féin have been described as "the title deeds of a revolution". When the idea of Sinn Féin was conceived, Ireland was awakening from the nightmare of the nineteenth century, which had seen the Great Hunger, the millions forced to emigrate and the land war. But even in the midst of these horrors, some dared to dream of a different Ireland – a free Ireland.

The tragic fate of Parnell had shown the limits of a so-called constitutional nationalism that depended on the good will of British political parties or British governments to grant as concessions the inalienable rights of the Irish people. The most important principle of Sinn Féin was and is self-reliance. Only the people of this island can secure our liberation and mould our society to suit our unique heritage, our character, our economic needs and our place in the wider world. That was the core value of the fledgling Sinn Féin. That is still true today. And from the beginning, while always asserting that the end of the union was in the interests of all the people of this island, Sinn Féin extended a hand of friendship to unionists.

This Sinn Féin policy was outlined by Arthur Griffith at the first convention in the Rotunda in November 1905. "For the Orangeman of the North, ceasing to be the blind instrument of his own as well as his fellow-countrymen's destruction, we have the greeting of brotherhood, as for the nationalist of the South, long taught to measure himself by English standards and save the face of tyranny by sending Irishmen to sit impotently in a foreign legislature whilst it forges the instruments of his oppression."

It was a time of renewal and rebirth in Ireland. Sinn Féin was the political expression of that dream, which blossomed in Conradh na Gaeilge, Cumann Lúthchleas Gael, the trade union movement, na Fianna Éireann, the cooperative movement, the development of Irish industries and agriculture, Inghinidhe na hÉireann, Cumann na mBan, the movement for women's suffrage, and the Irish Women Workers' Union of Ireland. Women played a key role in these developments despite resistance from some of their male comrades. It was a woman, Máire de Buitléir, who first proposed the name Sinn Féin for the new political movement. Jennie Wyse Power was Sinn Féin's treasurer from 1908 and became vice-president of Sinn Féin in 1911. Constance Markievicz, minister for labour in the First Dáil, was one of the first women cabinet ministers in the world. Margaret Buckley was president of Sinn Féin from 1937 to 1950.

The first Constitution of Sinn Féin simply stated that its first objective was "the re-establishment of the independence of Ireland". Political events soon required a clearer definition of what that independence would mean. The political pendulum had swung toward constitutional nationalism. Irish hopes rested once more on the good will of a British political party. The Irish

Parliamentary Party at Westminster reduced the national demand for freedom to the polite request for limited Home Rule within the British Empire. But even this was not conceded as the British government acted, as always, first and last, in its own interest. It was Tory England, in alliance with Irish unionism, that brought the gun into Irish politics in the twentieth century – not republicans, not the Irish Volunteers, not Sinn Féin. With the Tory-unionist gun came the concept of partition. In the words of James Connolly, the republican who most clearly defined what the dream of a free, just and equal Ireland should be, they placed Ireland upon the dissecting table.

I consciously use the word dream because that is how many great ventures are first conceived, whether in our personal lives or in the wider scheme of things. The dream is important, but the big challenge is to make the dream a reality, to make the dream come true.

And so the political pendulum swung back towards that element in Irish politics which, since the days of the United Irishmen, had always demanded national sovereignty and an Irish republic. There were many republicans involved in the formation of Sinn Féin. They played a pivotal role in founding the Irish Volunteers. Many of them actively supported the workers in the Great Lockout of 1913 in Dublin. This was a great period of debate, of exchanges of ideas as leaders and thinkers and activists, dreamers all, met and influenced each other. It was the time when the tributaries of separatism, anti-sectarianism, feminism, cultural revival, socialism and the physical force tradition flowed into the river of Irish republicanism.

The result was the 1916 Rising and the Proclamation of the Irish Republic, the founding document of modern Irish republicanism and a charter of liberty with international as well as national importance. In it, the republic guarantees religious and civil liberty, equal rights and equal opportunities to all its citizens; the Proclamation contains a commitment to cherish all the children of the nation equally. Its anti-sectarianism is evident in the words "oblivious of the differences carefully fostered by an alien government, which have divided a minority from the majority in the past". And at a time when women in most countries did not have the vote, the government of this new republic was to be elected by the suffrage of all her men and women.

These are not just clever words or empty rhetoric. This was the dream taking shape. These are great words, great ideas, which it is our task – our responsibility – to see implemented. These words are a promise to every Irish citizen that she and he can share in the dignity of human kind, as equals with equal opportunity. That we can enjoy freedom, educate our children, provide for our families and not exploit our neighbours. Those who most immediately understood the significance of the Proclamation were revolutionary Irish women. One of these, Margaret Skinnider, was wounded during the fighting in Dublin in Easter week. Afterward she said: ". . . we had the same right to risk our lives as the men; that in the Constitution of the Irish republic, women were on an equality with men. For the first time in history indeed, a Constitution had been written that incorporated the principle of equal suffrage." This view was echoed by Hanna Sheehy-Skeffington, who said: "It was the first time in history that men fighting for freedom voluntarily included women."

The British suppressed the Rising, court-martialled and executed the leaders and imprisoned many of the insurgents. Many of them stood as candidates on a Sinn Féin and abstentionist ticket in the elections of 1918. The Irish people endorsed the republic in this election. Sinn Féin won a clear majority, and instead of taking their seats in the British Parliament, Dáil Éireann, an all-Ireland parliament, was established. In 1919 the Dáil declared the independence of the republic and published its "Message to the Free Nations of the World" and the "Democratic Programme". From this high water mark of united national resistance, republicans faced a bloody war with the British, who suppressed the Dáil. A truce was called in July 1921 to facilitate negotiations. A counter-revolution and the establishment by the British of two states with their own parliaments followed.

Those who established Sinn Féin 100 years ago, those who fought in 1916 and later against the might of the British Empire, and those who raised the flag of resistance in each subsequent generation did so in circumstances that differed and changed as the years rolled past. This is not 1905. It is 2005. It is the twenty-first century. If Irish republicanism is to be relevant in modern Ireland, it needs to be defined and redefined. Republicanism today, and our dream, our vision of the future, draws on our historic roots and the rights of the Irish people. It also reflects our contemporary experience and the inspiration provided by the heroes of this phase of struggle – people like Maire Drumm and Bobby Sands, Eddie Fullerton and Sheena Campbell, John Davey and many others.

Sinn Féin is an Irish republican party. Our strategy to achieve a united, independent Ireland marks us out from other Irish political parties. Our primary political objectives are an end to partition, an end to the union, the construction of a new national democracy, a new republic on the island of Ireland and reconciliation between Orange and Green. But we are not prepared to wait until we have achieved these goals for people to have their rights to a decent home, to a job and a decent wage, to decent public services like health and education, and a safer, cleaner environment. The big task facing us while we struggle for these other objectives is to play a full part in bringing the peace process to completion. That has to be the priority of all responsible political parties. That is a difficult and challenging task. The Good Friday Agreement of 1998 was the biggest step forward in this process.

Beyond the Agreement, which is essentially an accommodation, Irish republicanism has a vision of a new society, a new Ireland, that is democratic. That is economic as well as political: a society which is inclusive of all citizens, in which there is a redistribution of wealth for the well-being of the aged, for the advancement of youth, for the liberation of women and the protection of our children. It foresees a new relationship between these islands, resting upon our mutual independence and mutual respect. From the beginning, saving the Irish language from extinction and reviving our national language has been a key aim of Sinn Féin. Pádraig Pearse recognised that without Conradh na Gaeilge there would not have been a revolution in Ireland.

Our republicanism has to be about change – fundamental, deep-rooted change. It has to be about creating the conditions whereby people are empowered to make that change. Key to achieving this is the hard, tedious, difficult work of building political strength. By building that strength, we will build the capacity to move both the British and the Irish governments and the unionists and to influence the political agenda. Sinn Féin is now politically and organisationally stronger than at any time since the 1920s. We have developed new approaches. We have taken difficult and risky decisions. We have demonstrated time and time again a preparedness to go on the political offensive, to take initiatives and go toe to toe with our political opponents in the battle of ideas, as well as in the hard job of building workable political partnerships. All of these facts give some explanation of why we are almost perpetually at the centre of a political storm. Our political opponents, and even those who should be our allies in the struggle for Irish freedom and peace, fear our growing electoral strength. It is amazing to watch the feverish efforts of other parties rushing to claim their republican and Sinn Féin roots while attacking and condemning us.

We have no fear of that. If Labour, Fianna Fáil, Fine Gael, the SDLP and the rest want to be republican, then Sinn Féin welcomes that. The more the merrier. We have no monopoly on republicanism. What is a republican if not someone who strives for Irish freedom and justice and an end to partition? The success of our party – and the test for all other parties – has to be about how much change they secure and how much progress they make in improving the life of citizens and in achieving national freedom. We also have a lot of work to do. We don't pretend to have all the answers.

Sinn Féin is accused of recognising the Army Council of the IRA as the legitimate government of this island. That is not the case.

The supreme governing and legislative body of Sinn Féin is the Ard Fheis. This annual conference is where our party makes our big decisions. It is the supreme authority of our party. This is where we elect our leadership, agree our policies and set in place our strategies. I do not believe that the Army Council is the government of Ireland. Such a government will only exist when all the people of this island elect it. Does Sinn Féin accept the institutions of the southern state as the legitimate institutions of this state? Of course we do. But we are critical of these institutions. We are entitled to be. We want to change them, to improve them, peacefully and democratically.

The freedom won by those who gave their lives in 1916 and in other periods has been squandered by others who attained political power on their backs. Apart from our criticism of the institutions themselves, the reality is that they are partitionist, and we want to see not only better institutions but an open, transparent government representative of all the people of this island – and we make no apologies for that. Do we accept partition? No, we do not accept partition. Do we accept British rule in our country? No, we do not. Do we want a united Ireland? Yes, we do.

This book argues that we must use our mandate to build an island-wide, a nationwide, mass Sinn Féin movement. Our goal has to be to have a Sinn Féin cumann in every electoral ward across Ireland. We have to open our party up to women comrades and to people who will bring their own life experiences and values. We have to learn to work in partnership with other parties, and people of a like mind, to construct a network, an alliance for unity, which will act as a catalyst for real change – a coalition for unity which brings people and parties with a similar vision of the future together.

When people elect us they expect us to do all in our power to implement our policies. That entails participating in government if we have the mandate and if the opportunity presents. If we can secure an inter-party agreement that is consistent with our republican principles and objectives, that would allow us to bring about real change, then we should give such a prospect our very serious consideration. And that is exactly what Sinn Féin is committed to doing. A special Ard Fheis, a full delegate conference, will determine our position, our course of action. It is our members who will take that decision and no one else.

Our party is about bringing about change right across this island. Equality is our watchword. We live in a prosperous country. There is sufficient wealth in our society to ensure that no one should want for any of the basics of life, yet a fifth of our people are living in poverty. We have a two-tier health system and a housing crisis. Our children are being educated in dilapidated and run-down school buildings. There is no sign of decent childcare services. At every turn, punitive measures are taken against the disadvantaged. We are prepared to work with others who share our vision of a fair and equitable society that provides real solutions, not broken promises.

Sinn Féin wants to change the *status quo,* not to join it. We should not be judged by how many cabinet seats we get or indeed how many votes we get, although that is a crucial part of building political strength. The measure of our success can only be judged by the amount of change we bring about. Without political strength, you cannot bring about change. But having built that strength, the real test is how to use it to improve society. Other parties have been in government, some for decades, but they have failed to bring about the changes which the majority of people desire and deserve. That is why the Sinn Féin vote is growing.

What Sinn Féin is trying to do at this time is unprecedented. While dealing with the ongoing challenges of the peace process, we are continuing to build for Irish unity and independence, at the same time preparing to be in government in the future. But we want social and economic change in the here and now. We want equality now. So, we are also building a political party right across all thirty-two counties. We are building a campaigning party and building political strength and alliances with others to bring about the changes now, by trying to set the political agenda so that those in government have to respond, even if they are not happy to do so.

Sinn Féin will be in government in the north in the time ahead. But we will only consider coalition in the south if that advances the process of change and the struggle for equality. We have no interest in ministerial seats for the sake of it. And we certainly could not embrace, never mind support, the punitive anti-people measures which the conservative parties advocate. Neither could we proceed without a real strategy for Irish unity.

With the developing peace process, growing concern over globalisation and crisis in Europe, we are at a strategic crossroads in Ireland. We need to decide on the type of country we want and what we want its place in the world to be. The current consensus is failing communities throughout Ireland and making no impact on the international stage. We need to stop this drift, we need a battle of ideas, and we need action to deliver change. I hope that this book will help concentrate debate – the battle of ideas – something which is lacking in Irish society in 2005. Far from being over, there are many ideological battles to be fought: making peace with unionism, ending partition, distribution of wealth, elimination of poverty, protection of public services, the European Union, reform of the UN and many, many more.

Irish republicans have demonstrated time and time again our capacity to overcome adversity and advance our struggle for freedom and justice against enormous odds. It is not enough to repeat slogans. We are not verbal republicans or rhetorical revolutionaries. We are carrying the honoured name of Sinn Féin into the twenty-first century. And after a century of struggle, it is right to ask, when will we get our united Ireland? When will Ireland have independence? There's only one answer to that. We will get it when our combined efforts, our combined strength, our determination make its achievement unstoppable. We will not settle for less. And the greater our efforts, the more quickly we will achieve our goals.

So, this book is a modest contribution to that effort. It was heavily influenced by the ideas and writings of Caroline Coleman, Robbie Smyth, Mícheál Mac Donncha, Anthony Coughlan, Matt Treacy, Shannonbrooke Murphy, Eoin Ó Broin, Eoghan Mac Cormaic, Jim Gibney, Mitchel McLaughlin, Ted Howell, Máirtín Ó Muilleoir, Lucilita Bhreatnach, Margaret Ward, Rita O'Hare, Caoilfhionn Ní Dhonabhain, Daltún Ó Ceallaigh, Shane Mac Tomais, Brian Carty, Laura Friel, and Seanna Walsh.

I thank them all. Any mistakes are mine.

I want also to thank Dawn Doyle who helped with editing and other chores, above and beyond the call of duty and Steve MacDonogh who relaxed his publisher's deadline (again). Richard

McAuley's help and patience as usual was indispensable. Without him this book would not have been written at this time. In conclusion I want to thank Colette and our family for their support. *Tá mé buioch daoibh go léir.*

Gerry Adams
August 2005

Chapter 1

IRISH REPUBLICANISM

Why am I a republican? Why indeed? Would I be a republican if my life had been moulded differently? Truth to tell, I don't know. All of us are influenced by our upbringing, by the conditions in which we live and by our experiences. So I am who I am because of all this, and my politics and beliefs are the result of that.

So what are these beliefs? My first basic belief is that people should be free. In this consumer age of the twenty-first century, what does that mean? It means people should be treated as equals. When I was younger, I had a fairly simplistic notion of all this. In my teens, I came to a realisation that I and my peers were not being treated equally. At first I thought that maybe this was because we had been overlooked. I knew we are all guilty at times of treating others unfairly. This is often because of bad temper, or by way of reprisal, or because of bad feeling or thoughtlessness. But I could not see why anyone would want to treat anyone unfairly as a matter of policy. Even as I came to a consciousness of how embedded the unfairness was where I lived, I thought it was only a matter of bringing this to the attention of the people in charge. As soon as the powers that be realised the problem, they would rectify matters. So my reasoning went.

But then I came to realise that the powers that be are the

powers that be because of the unfairness. They are unlikely to want to change that. Or if they do, they are likely only to change it in a way or to a degree which allows them to remain in charge. Nowadays, I consider this to be part of the human condition. People have power or the illusion or the symbols of power, and they are loath to give these up. Or people are used to things being done in a certain way, and they are slow to change it or to believe that they could change it if they wanted. Some people are reluctant to even consider that change is possible. So for me, politics has to be about empowering people. If politics do not empower people then they are useless. People have to belong. They have to have a stake in society and in their communities. They have to be cherished, and their humanity has to be respected and defended. People have rights and entitlements. Their human dignity has to be acknowledged and upheld.

I am instinctively against empires. Of any kind. Political or religious, secular or industrial. Empires are bad. They are all about power for elites, and I am against power for elites. I am for power for the masses and rights for the individual. People have to be sovereign. Monarchies are an insult to humankind. I cannot consent to be ruled by such a system. People are citizens, not subjects. One thing which I have come to value more and more is a basic belief in people. In my experience, most people are decent. Given a choice, the vast majority of people will do the decent thing. But human behaviour is hugely influenced by the conditions in which we live. Some people have very limited life choices because of their race, gender, social status, educational limitations, disability or poverty. Their entire lives, even in the Ireland of the Celtic Tiger, especially if they are women, are spent seeking the basics for living, so they spend their lives trying to survive or trying to ensure that their families survive.

This is grossly unfair. There are certain rights which people require if they are to have the basics for living, including the right to food, to water, to a home and work and to health and education services. Society must be shaped around these rights. Society must be shaped around people – citizens – not elites, monarchies or hierarchies.

The people of Ireland have the right to self-government and the right to have maximum control of that government. No British politician could ever govern Ireland in Irish interests. That is not his or her function or purpose. British ministers rule, under-standably enough, in the interests of the British government. These interests are not in the best interest of the people of Ireland. How could they be? Partition is not in the best interests of the people of Ireland. The partition of this island is immoral and illegitimate. If these matters were guided by any yardstick of jus-tice or decency, the partition of Ireland would be undone and the union would be ended. But life is not like that; life is unfair. But the fact that, in many instances, the unfairness is because of society should be a cause for hope, because history teaches us that soci-eties can be changed. Not too long ago slavery was accepted, as was the disenfranchisement of women. Discrimination was legal. Apartheid was once the order of the day in South Africa. No longer. Germany has been reunited. The USSR is no more.

Change in society hardly ever comes of its own accord; it has to be engineered. This is rarely accomplished without struggle or sacrifice. But it is important that we know that one person can make a difference. Why make the effort if we think it will have no effect? If we believe that one person cannot make a difference, why would any of us try to do anything? I also believe in the power of positive thinking. People's expectations of their own worth should be raised, not lowered. Problems should be seen as chal-lenges. Nothing is impossible. Whoever it was that described pol-itics as the art of the possible was reducing politics to a mediocre trade. Politics has to be much more than that. Who has the right to decide what is possible – political elites or citizens? No citizen should be excluded.

Politics is often seen as the stuff of parliamentary partisan pol-iticking, of soundbites and illusion, of strokes and favours, patron-age and cronyism. Little wonder many people say, "I have no interest in politics." Little wonder fewer and fewer people bother to vote. They obviously see no value in their vote. They think they can make no real difference. In whose interest is this? This alien-ation works for the elites, who know that politics affects every

aspect of our lives. Decisions over how we live and the quality of our lives are political decisions. Why should we give up our right to have a say in that? Decisions over the lives of our children and their future should not be surrendered to others. Citizens have the right to be involved in all these matters. And politicans and other public servants must be accountable to their peers.

All of this is an argument for republican systems of government; that is, systems in which the people are sovereign and equal. Even if Ireland had not been colonised or partitioned, I would make this argument. It has become the core value of my political beliefs. It is at the centre of my world view and my opinion of how all people should be treated. Such a society has to be tolerant. Citizens have to learn and to be encouraged to be tolerant of each other and of views, opinions or beliefs which are different from ours. Society must reflect and include the entirety of its people, not part of them. Inclusivity is vital to the well-being of any community, whether a nation community, the global village or a local populace. Why should gender be the basis for the exclusion of anyone? Or disability? Why should race or class or skin colour or creed give one group of human beings the ability to deny other human beings their full rights or entitlements as citizens?

And if citizens have rights, why are they not all-encompassing rights? Should the right to the basics of life not include economic rights as well as political and social rights? If society is a two-tiered one in which people are subjects, that is how people will be treated. As subjects they will be afforded only such concessions as the privileged deem adequate for them. They will be denied citizens' rights. This is unacceptable. All human beings have the right, as a birthright, to be treated equally. Citizens have responsibilities. These include an obligation to contribute to society. In my experience, most people are prepared to do this. Civic and public service are a necessary part of the obligations of citizenship. I believe this should be inculcated into our education as part of teaching the core values, obligations and responsibilities of citizens and the state.

An empowered people are an educated people. An educated people are an empowered people. A rights-based society requires citizens to fulfil their obligations for the common good. It also requires the state to inform all citizens of their rights, and to uphold and defend these rights. All this is politics, but it is politics of a different order. It is the politics of a rights-based, citizen-centred society. It is entirely within our grasp, if this is what we want, to reorganise our society in this way.

Ireland today is a country in transition. There have been many positive developments in both states on the island. A lot of the old certainties have gone. A lot of the old conservative influences have been weakened. A lot of unfinished business still has to be completed, but progress has been made. Yes, Ireland remains partitioned and the British continue to uphold the union, and there are deep and profound issues which need to be resolved between unionism and the rest of us. But no one should minimise how much our society has changed, particularly in this last forty years or so. In particular, the experience of the Twenty-Six Counties from the 1920s to today has been an incredible journey. When the state was established, there was little effort made to build a society that had the potential to deliver on the aspirations of Connolly and Pearse, or one that could aspire to the objectives of the 1916 Proclamation and the 1919 Democratic Programme. These principles were abandoned by many of its political leaders who failed to deliver on the potential of the Irish revolution.

The result was that one out of every two people born here between 1920 and 1990 left the state to find work and a better future somewhere else. That is a damning statistic. The Twenty-Six Counties is a state which has never been able to house all of it is citizens, or able to educate them adequately or equitably. In fact, in nearly every measure, in almost every facet of life and society – from healthcare, transport, economic development, the treatment of young, old and women – the state failed. The new elite which managed the new state was also narrow-minded and repressive. They chose a conservative, often sectarian definition of what Ireland could be. Between 1923 and 1953, the very artistic spirit that had fuelled a generation of revolutionaries only decades before was actively censored.

There were few parts of political life where the new state's government was not prepared to intervene. It lost no time in establishing the Censorship of Films Act, under which the film censor banned large numbers of films and cut scenes from others. Then, under the Censorship of Publications Act, books by almost every writer of note were banned, and a great many magazines were also banned. The cultural renaissance in music, sport, literature and art in the late nineteenth and early twentieth century was sidelined. Then there was the rewriting of the education system with lip-service to Irish, which was turned into a parody of rural Ireland. Successive governments failed to put together a language policy, even to this day.

Political life in the Twenty-Six Counties was dominated by the rivalry between Fine Gael and Fianna Fáil, the two post-revolutionary elites. But as the immediate effects of the Civil War receded and partitionism set in, this rivalry turned out not to be about any big ideological issue. It was over who could wield the symbols of state and control the spoils of power. Both these parties conformed with a conservative definition of the national project and agreed on the need to stymie the emergence of any class-based or radical politics. It was a simple but very workable thesis. Little quarter was given to ideological or class-based politics. The result was that the normal left/right split found in the political party systems across Europe was absent here. Instead, the state was rooted in political conservatism, religious fundamentalism and preservation of the *status quo*. The new regime retained the old colonial banking system and much of the old court and legal processes. There would be some reform of the worst excesses of local government, but ultimately the real agenda was to centralise even more power in their own hands. Even today local government systems on this island have the least funding and exercise less power than any other local authority system in Europe.

The new state also handed over control of the fledgling education system to the Catholic and Protestant churches. They allowed and endorsed a deliberate backtracking on the ideals of the republic declared in 1916. Instead, the Catholic Hierarchy's conservatism now fuelled a new counter-revolutionary zeal. This new state was one where trade unionists were denounced from the pulpit, their offices attacked by mobs in the streets; where communists, republicans and anyone else who challenged the *status quo* were deemed enemies of the state. All of this encouraged a growing neurosis, which led to patronage and corrupt political practices that are still being exposed today.

Of course, there was opposition to all this, and there were battles waged on many fronts by those who wanted a different society. But despite their efforts, the old order prevailed. However, what the state couldn't stall for ever was the impact of the outside world and the effect it would have on a subdued people. Interestingly, it was the late 1950s television, with its news reports and imported TV programmes, which brought new values and lifestyles into Irish homes: pictures and reports of a western world in considerable turmoil with civil rights protests in the American south, war in Vietnam, revolutions in Latin America, as well as the new music and youth culture emerging in the northern and west coast cities of the United States.

By the end of the 1960s, more than 70 per cent of RTÉ's content was imported international programmes. There was a clear dichotomy between the values and morals of conservative, traditional Ireland and the new liberal, secular values of British and American TV programming. There was a resurgence of interest in the writings and teachings of the leaders of 1916 at the time of the fiftieth anniversary of the Rising. Women also were campaigning for basic rights. The media provided a platform for these causes. The effect of all this was not calming, and not homogenous, and when it showed civil rights protests on the streets of Derry and Belfast in 1968, it woke Irish public opinion.

For a time it seemed that all would be swept before these reborn movements. The north was in turmoil. Fianna Fáil was convulsed, its supporters openly sympathetic to the plight of nationalists in the Six Counties, and Jack Lynch's government was caught up in the crisis. But Fianna Fáil slowly steadied itself and moved back into the symbolism of a more vocal but otherwise ineffectual rhetorical nationalism. The renewed interest in radical or leftist politics benefited the Labour Party, which then allowed itself to be sucked into a conservative and reactionary Fine Gael government. The women's movement was marginalised and isolated with drip-fed, piecemeal reforms. And all the while, the situation in the north deteriorated and slipped deeper and deeper into open warfare, with no strategy from the southern establishment other than that of cooperation with the British.

Looking back now, it is hard to imagine the journey that the economy and its workers, their families and communities have travelled through over the last eighty-five years while all this was going on. From a republican point of view, the ideals enshrined in the Proclamation, the Democratic Programme and the works of Pearse, Connolly and others were never delivered on, whether these were the promise to cherish all of the children of the nation equally or the commitments to ensure that the wealth of the nation was used for the people's interests and not for private and personal gain. The economic life of the Twenty-Six County state is one that moved from trying and failing to breathe life into a rural-based economy, followed by the emergence of protectionist economic policies aimed at stimulating local industry, through to encouraging multinational firms to site here. The decision to join the EEC was pivotal. Now, over thirty years later, as Sinn Féin and others predicted at that time, the state is poised to enter a new political union with the European Union.

If this chapter had been written twenty years ago, it would have been about an economy that was on the margin and dipping towards failure, debt ridden, stagnant and suffering from the amputation that partition wreaked on it. But all is changed utterly, and now we have an economy that, per capita, is one of the wealthiest in the world. This economic success is the result of a series of related factors. The first one was the realisation within the economic development agencies that radical surgery was needed in their own economic strategising. In the mid 1980s, they recognised that what we now consider the old industries of ship building, steel, car making and textiles would not be the core economic activity of the future.

They focused their attentions on four strategic sectors: pharmaceuticals, financial services, the then new information and communication technologies and finally the food processing industry.

Other factors taken into consideration in planning were the amount of spare capacity for growth, especially in terms of an educated available work-force; cheap infrastructure, particularly electricity; and an economy where, because of years of recession, there was also a huge untapped scope for growth. Finally, there was the offer to investors of unprecedented tax breaks, fast planning decisions and generous grants to firms who would site here.

The developing EU offered a tariff-free marketplace in Europe, and the American companies based here could import product back into the US without levies or tariffs either. We had managed to get the best of both worlds. At the same time, it meant we were abandoning even the pretence of investing in rural Ireland, and economic resources and wealth were sucked into the cities and the east coast. Finally, there was the workforce, educated, diligent and desperate for secure employment and prepared to abandon most union-based work conditions for unheard-of job security.

Then, as economic activity surged in the 1990s, the Irish media finally found a voice to tell the public about the scale and extent of corruption in Ireland. A scandalised populace learned that *their* state was one where politicians sold political power, taking decisions based on the interests of the wealthy. There seemed to be no end to this political and corporate corruption affecting planning, economic policies, government procurement, banking. Then came perhaps the saddest and most damning revelations: of the systematic abuse of our children and women in state institutions.

Herein lie other reasons why I am a republican. Historically, republican opposition to the British state and its local administration was rooted in an analysis that the British were making decisions about Ireland where the British interest came first and last. This goes to the core of republicanism since the 1790s. Then the local Anglo ascendancy were effectively running a political franchise under licence from the British state, but in their interests too. There was economic mismanagement on a large scale. The early writings of Theobald Wolfe Tone and others return repeatedly to this point.

Fast forward into the Ireland of the present day and history's unlearnt lessons have meant a return to the previous century's economic reality. The Ireland of today, like that of 200 years ago, has international forces which make demands in the local economy in both economic and political life. We also have, as in the time of Grattan's Parliament, a domestic elite which is corrupt and wholly self-interested. For me, all this is an argument for genuine republicanism. There is also the big question: who we are building this economy for?

The Twenty-Six Counties of today is a place where at least one in four children lives in poverty, where one in five students leaves school without a second-level qualification, where one in four adults has literacy difficulties, where a simple trip to work can take hours, where ill health could means days languishing in a hospital waiting room, where looking after your children means incurring massive financial costs while you work, where adults work long hours simply to be able to afford housing, where the gap between rich and poor is, next to the USA, the most unequal in the industrialised world.

The health of the state cannot be measured only by how much wealth it produces. The real test is in how that wealth is used for the benefit of citizens. The real test is the equality one. While much progress has been made, this state fails that test – miserably. Into this equation have come two new factors: one is the momentum for political change created by the peace process and the other is the new multiculturalism driven not by invasion and conquest, as in the past, but by the power of economic forces.

The peace process has shown that a better republic, a genuine all-Ireland republic, more equal and fair, is possible; that we can roll back the decades of political failure in the Twenty-Six Counties and in the Six Counties and build a new Ireland. It will be a changing Ireland into which thousands of new Irish will bring new ideas, new ways of thinking to our shores, challenging us to show that we can build a truly inclusive society and set about righting the inequalities that pervade our society today. It will see a lasting peace between Orange and Green, not in the context of a partitioned Ireland but in a democratic republic in a united Ireland.

Is this possible? I think it is. That's why I am an Irish republican.

Chapter 2

THE ROAD MAP TO
A UNITED IRELAND

I was born in Belfast in 1948 into a working-class republican family. While I had no political consciousness until my teens, as is I suppose natural for most people, from quite an early age I did have a sense of national consciousness. Looking back on it now, I consider this to be a blessing. When I was five or six, a hurling stick was placed into my hand, and I trailed after older cousins to hurling and Gaelic football games in the Falls Park. This sense of the Gaeldom was reinforced by Christian Brothers from Munster. For a brief period when I was ten, I boxed for a club on the Shankill Road. That was 1958. My Uncle Dominic and Aunt Maggie lived in Dublin, and from my first all-Ireland football final with my Uncle Paddy in 1960, I was a frequent visitor to their home at Whitehall and in later years in Howth. I have always retained a great *grá* for Dublin city, for the Phoenix Park where we went on long rambles and for Howth Head. And, of course, Croke Park. Scholarship courses presided over by Irish language enthusiast Brother Beausang brought me to Gweedore and the Donegal Gaeltacht and the beginning of a lifelong affinity with the western highlands around Sliabh an Earagail. Teenage years brought me into youth hostelling and camping, the world of *fleadhs* and *céilis*, pub sessions and *sean nós* singing. So I was comfortable and rooted in my sense of Irishness.

When I attempted to subsidise these activities by seeking out a part-time job, I was rather surprised to be told that I "dug with the wrong fut". This was after being asked what school I went to (Saint Mary's was obviously a Catholic establishment), but the put-down was delivered without rancour, almost as a matter of fact.

When I started work in a public house, it was my first real contact with working-class unionists. They, too, had their sense of Irishness. In sing-songs in the back room, along with the popular tunes of the time, standards included "The Green Glens of Antrim", "The Boys from the County Armagh", "When Irish Eyes Are Smiling", "I'll Take You Home Again, Kathleen", and so on. Party songs, in this case Orange songs, like "The Sash", "The Green Grassy Slopes of the Boyne" or "The Boul' Orange Heroes of Comber", were usually sung only during the Orange marching season. On one occasion, I was moved to render a version of "The Sash" in Irish. A Somme veteran followed me with a rendition of "Kevin Barry". I have to say I was never offended by Orange songs delivered in this setting or spirit. They were generally sung in good humour and with much slagging. I had my own collection of Richard Hayward's Orange songs and could sing all of the above, and did so frequently at *scoraíocht* in houses on the Falls Road. This is not to suggest that these were the good old days and that everything was fine. Everything was not fine. As the civil rights campaigns began and my political consciousness developed, sectarianism laid by Ian Paisley and others was reasserting itself.

No matter that the people I sold drink to lived in exactly the same two-bedroomed, toilet-in-the-back-yard, no-bathroom, terraced house as me: their fears were roused by the demands for equality. This is not to say they were all sectarian; they patently were not. The year 1966 with its Easter Rising commemorations – banned in the north by the unionist government – saw the mobilisation of the B Specials (a part-time armed unionist paramilitary force). Seeing some of the shipyard men and other punters who bellied up to the bar for bottles of Guinness and half 'uns in their uniforms with holstered revolvers and batons gave me a different view of their world. Hurling, Croke Park, the Irish language were no part of it. They had a sense of empire which was the direct opposite of mine. We had so much in common and yet so much to polarise us. Later, when I moved to a different hostelry and as the situation continued to deteriorate, I met different unionists, professional people, journalists and the like, who journeyed to Dublin to support Ulster in the Rugby or Ireland as the case might be. In this drinking establishment, party songs were strictly forbidden and probably would not have been entertained by the clientele in any case. But in the strange schizophrenic world in which we live, it was here I first heard "The Ballad of Henry Joy McCracken", the United Irelander who was hanged in Belfast by the British for his part in the 1798 Uprising.

By now I was involved in republican politics. When the planners started the destruction of the Falls Road with the demolition of the Loney area – a district of densely packed houses at the bottom of the Falls Road – I and other republicans joined local people in protest at the construction of Divis Flats, a new slum. The civil rights movement slowly began to shine a light on the inequalities and injustices of the northern state. There was organised opposition to discrimination in housing, in employment, to a restricted franchise which saw many Catholics denied the right to vote, and to a local government structure and the Stormont Parliament which were entirely dominated by unionist politicians.

Change was also coming to Irish republicanism. The Wolfe Tone Society was established to provide a forum for discussion among republicans and others. It was James Connolly who said of Wolfe Tone that he united "the hopes of the new revolutionary faith and the ancient aspirations of an oppressed people". In the late 1960s as a young activist, I was coming to terms with these hopes and with the ancient aspirations. But our struggle was very much a defensive struggle. We were alienated from the state and denied the most fundamental rights even to politically organise. The work we did was of a basic though hugely important nature. Sinn Féin was banned. So was its newspaper. To succeed we needed to win the right to politically organise. We needed to identify the best in the republican tradition which we inherited and to develop republicanism to meet the needs of our own time. This is a constant task, as necessary in 2005 as at any other time. Irish republicanism is based on a number of core principles, which are as relevant today as they ever were. First and foremost, there is the commitment to the sovereignty of the people, to democracy in its fullest sense. There is the commitment to unity of Catholic, Protestant and Dissenter and the rejection of sectarianism of any kind. And there is the commitment to the unity of this island and its people, national self-determination, an end to partition and the establishment of a sovereign thirty-two county republic.

These are still the basic principles which motivate Irish republicans today. I would define a republican as someone who adheres to these principles and acts upon them. The term "republicans" is often used in a narrower sense to describe members and supporters of Sinn Féin. I think a broader definition is required which embraces all who share our commitment to the complete freedom of the Irish people.

Flowing naturally from the basic principles I have outlined are other commitments. Our historical experience gave us an affinity with other peoples who were struggling for national self-determination. Thus anti-imperialism and internationalism have been embraced by Irish republicans. Belief in what Pearse described as the sovereign people has led Irish republicans to develop our politics along the lines laid down by Pearse and Connolly, seeking social and economic democracy as well as national political democracy. Connolly's measurement of freedom, as expressed in 1915, is just as relevant today: "In the long run the freedom of a nation is measured by the freedom of its lowest class; every upward step of that class to the possibility of possessing higher things raises the standard of the nation in the scale of civilization." We cannot divorce these core republican principles from the struggle, which they have inspired.

Throughout almost thirty years of armed conflict, the British government sought unsuccessfully to defeat Irish republicanism politically and militarily. It waged a counter-insurgency war with the aim of isolating and eradicating organised republicanism. It could only hope to do so by attempting to intimidate the communities from which republicans draw our support. As well as direct occupation of nationalist districts by the British army and RUC, British forces used loyalist paramilitaries as auxiliaries in their war. This, of course, was met with resistance in many forms: armed struggle, civil disobedience, street campaigning, prison struggle, hunger strikes to the death, electoral politics, the mobilisation of international opinion and long and tortuous negotiations.

In many ways, while there were offensive phases of this period of struggle, the campaigns were still generally defensive. Throughout it all, a culture of resistance was developed. But it was when republicans moved to develop a culture of change that the struggles, in all their aspects, of the previous decades started to fit into a strategic context. Through building political alliances, through dialogue and debate, through engagement with our political opponents and with our political enemies, republicans helped to chart a course out of armed conflict and towards the peaceful resolution of the causes of conflict.

When the situation is most difficult, it is natural that people may feel that progress is impossible. That has not been my experience. Of course, it is very frustrating and challenging to be continuously prevented from making progress by way of great leaps forward which would justify the effort that is being made by those of us who want to bring about change. But sometimes history and struggle is like that. It is a process of incremental change. For example, in the late 1980s and early 1990s, Sinn Féin published a series of documents, including "A Scenario for Peace", "Pathway to Peace" and "Towards a Lasting Peace". At the height of the armed conflict, these publications were the culmination of a series of debates within Sinn Féin in which we dared to imagine what peace might look like from a republican perspective. At the time, others viewed peace and democracy as outside the remit of republicanism. They had a simplistic notion that getting "peace" was about defeating the IRA. Within this notion, the mechanisms for achieving peace became repression, exclusion and entrenchment.

Sinn Féin set about challenging those perceptions by creating an alternative ideological landscape. That meant republicans recapturing the use of the word peace and identifying peace not simply in terms of ending conflict, specifically the defeat of armed insurrection in the north of Ireland, but in terms of addressing the causes of that conflict. Peace meant justice. Clearly the mechanisms underpinning this understanding of peace were the polar opposite of the then established "security" agenda. Peace within these alternative terms of reference requires engagement, inclusion and progressive change, not repression and exclusion.

Republicans achieved this ideological shift by drawing upon established international notions of conflict resolution, especially the South African experience, and developing that insight with a more specific analysis of the historic and contemporary causes of conflict between Britain and Ireland, unionists and nationalists. Sinn Féin also engaged other elements of nationalist opinion in this emerging understanding as a means of developing a consensus, most particularly during the Hume/Adams initiative. We sought a collective understanding of the problem to further empower nationalist Ireland to challenge established British and unionist perceptions and resolutions.

Republicans also began a process of engagement with the British and Irish state which moved forward from secret meetings to public initiatives. The eventual defeat of the Tory government in 1997 and the election of a new Labour administration to the British Parliament freed the British government from some of the baggage of the former Thatcher/Major governments and gave a further impetus to this process. The Good Friday Agreement arose out of all of this and was made possible by a series of republican initiatives, most significantly the IRA cessation of August 1994, as well as the wider popular appeal of Sinn Féin's peace strategy and the party's growing electoral strength.

The Agreement is an historic compromise between nationalists, unionists, republicans, and the British and Irish governments. It is surely not the republic. But it is based on the principle of equality and it thus provides a route to further progress towards our republican objectives. The Good Friday Agreement has been described as an agreement to a journey but not to a destination.

Insofar as the constitutional question, that is the national question, is concerned, this is the case. However, the destination in respect of equality in all its dimensions – human rights; acceptable, accountable and representative policing; a fair and effective legal and judicial system – is well signposted. There are no ifs, ands or buts about it. Nor is there any question about the all-Ireland architecture of the political institutions agreed. With or without the Agreement, there is a responsibility on both governments to ensure these issues are speedily dealt with.

Clearly the Good Friday Agreement does not deliver the kind of aspirations envisaged by the United Irishmen, the Easter Rising or countless generations of republicans since then. But it does fundamentally change the nature and exercise of British sovereignty in the north. It also holds potential mechanisms to advance democratic goals. Constitutional changes within the Good Friday Agreement have been interpreted by different people in different ways. Some unionists have interpreted it as copper-fastening unionist "consent" and in that way upholding the unionist veto over the constitutional position of the north. Sinn Féin views the unionist veto as a negative mechanism that has undoubtedly encouraged unionist intransigence and a lack of engagement with the rest of us. Historically, it was the mechanism by which the British initially imposed partition, and since then it has allowed a national minority to impede the progress of the Irish nation as a whole.

Other interpretations of constitutional changes within the Agreement have recognised that while it may currently uphold the unionist veto, it also reduces the British territorial claim to that one hinge. Republicans have noted that the status of the north depends on "the consent of a majority of the people" and not on the consent of the majority of the unionist people. If a majority consensus for reunification emerges within the north, the British government is committed to abiding by the "wish expressed by a majority", and the north of Ireland would "cease to be part of the United Kingdom and form part of a united Ireland". There are already clear indications that, even within their own terms, the unionist claim of a majority status may become increasingly precarious. But Sinn Féin sees no reason to wait for a numerical nationalist majority to emerge in the north. Republicans remain confident that with the full implementation of the Good Friday Agreement, an end to institutionalised sectarianism and discrimination, and the creation of a level political playing field, it is possible to persuade a section of unionism to dare to imagine a united Ireland which would be to their advantage, a shared Ireland not simply shaped by republicans and nationalists but by unionists also.

One of the lost opportunities of the current peace process has been the failure of the British government to develop its role as persuaders for the Agreement rather than simply opting to be defenders of unionist interests. One of Sinn Féin's objectives in the negotiations that led to the Good Friday Agreement was to seek fundamental political and constitutional change. Sinn Féin believes that securing the repeal of the Government of Ireland Act and, in doing so, ending the absolutism of British territorial claims has undoubtedly weakened part of the union by limiting its duration to that decided by the will of a majority in the north. Of course, we reject completely any British government claim to jurisdiction in any part of Ireland. The union is wrong and will be until it ends. *Sin é.* But there is now no absolute commitment, no raft of parliamentary acts to back up an absolute claim. Now there is only an agreement to stay until a majority decides otherwise. And a majority means just that: 50 per cent plus one.

Irish unity does not just mean territorial unity. Ireland was united under British rule up to 1920, but political independence and the sovereignty of the people were denied. The British government should address this democratic imperative by becoming persuaders for Irish unity and by developing policies to end partition and end its jurisdiction in Ireland.

Sinn Féin seeks a representative democracy in a politically independent and reunited Ireland. This is the public position of other parties, including Fianna Fáil and the SDLP. This being the case, then it is surely in the best interests of all of us to sit down and debate and agree on a strategy for Irish reunification. More than eighty years have passed since the First Dáil was established in Dublin, but in all this time no Irish government has ever produced a green paper on Irish unity. No Irish government has ever set out a strategy, produced an outline of a legislative programme or an economic analysis, or set out the actions that would give effect to Irish unity.

I believe that there is a responsibility on the Irish government to bring forward a strategy to achieve national self-determination, Irish reunification, political independence, sovereignty and national reconciliation. There is an onus on Dublin to promote, popularise and seek support for this; to move the British government to become persuaders for a united Ireland; and to engage with unionists at all levels of society towards this end. Among the practical steps that could be taken are: the Irish government should bring forward a green paper on Irish unity; the work of the all-Ireland Ministerial Council should be expanded and additional all-Ireland Implementation Bodies created; Westminster MPs elected in the Six Counties should be accorded membership of the Dáil; and voting rights in presidential elections should be extended to citizens in the Six Counties.

Nationalists throughout Ireland also need to come to terms with the reality that the achievement of the national and democratic aim of Irish reunification will mean profound change. The political landscape will be transformed. New political alignments will evolve. A new multicultural society, embracing and respecting all traditions, must emerge. New island-wide economics will develop. There will be new demands on the economy to meet the needs of a reunited island and people. There will be many challenges but also many opportunities. Part of this opportunity will lie in discovering and exploiting the great potential for economic growth and development that an all-Ireland economy offers. The separation of two economies, duplication of services, competing strategies and two currencies have all negatively impacted on the economy.

We believe that a unified, all-Ireland economy holds out substantial potential for sustainable economic growth across the island through the development and coordination of economic planning on an all-Ireland basis. Strengthened economic growth is something which we all desire, and it is a persuasive argument in support of Irish unity. There are no historical inevitabilities that relieve any of us of our responsibility. It is up to those of us who believe in a united Ireland to make that case and persuade those people who do not. One of the ways we can do that is by setting out how we see Irish unity coming about and the type of society we envisage in a united country.

Consultation, engagement, persuasion and negotiation with a view to securing active support for a united Ireland must be the means towards these ends. By definition, this must involve all of the people of this island and their political representatives, the churches, civic society and the voluntary sector. It must involve a negotiation with the British government and be underpinned by a substantial peace dividend from both governments. Such a strategy must involve popular and political opinion in Britain, the international community and especially the European Union, the USA and former colonies whose success in securing political independence we seek to emulate.

Can we succeed? I believe we can. Pádraig Pearse asked in his poem "The Fool":

> O wise men riddle me this: what if the dream come true?
> What if the dream come true? And if millions unborn shall
>   dwell
> In the house that I shaped in my heart, the noble house of
>   my thought?

Making this dream come true has not been easy. But things have changed – profoundly – especially in the mindset of this generation of nationalists and republicans. The building of Sinn Féin as a party across the island of Ireland and our ability to make alliances with others is a crucial part of the road map to a united Ireland. So, too, is our willingness and ability to find accommodations with unionism. Unionism is part of our shared history. So is Orangeism. Orange is one of our national colours. The challenge is to join Orange and Green together.

Chapter 3

IRISH REPUBLICANISM IN THE TWENTY-FIRST CENTURY

In the opening line of the diary he kept during the first two weeks of his hunger strike, Bobby Sands wrote: "I am standing on the threshold of another trembling world."

As Sinn Féin celebrates our first 100 years, Irish republicanism stands on the threshold of great change, of many difficult challenges and great opportunities, and the possibility of achieving the united, independent, free Ireland previous generations have struggled for.

In looking at Irish republicanism in the twenty-first century, I want to consider some key issues in our partitioned Ireland that strike me as relevant to bringing about Ireland's reunification and the new Ireland we seek to build. To do this I am setting aside the specifics of the current peace process and looking beyond this to the longer-term prospects of, and challenges facing, Irish republicanism in the twenty-first century.

The key to building the new Ireland, however the people democratically shape it, is to start now. The process of change will itself lead to the new Ireland. We want a national republic which delivers the highest standard of services and protections to all citizens equally, guaranteeing parity of esteem and equality of treatment, opportunity and outcome.

This means ensuring that everyone is valued in society and that all citizens have the opportunity to make the greatest possible contribution to the Irish nation. It means that human potential is recognised and not marginalised, excluded or wasted. To achieve this obviously requires the full mobilisation of social resources.

This involves an ideological shift away from the conservatism of the Establishment. It means converting those resources which are currently given over to private profit making so that they can be utilised for social problem solving. Innovation needs to be encouraged, but to accomplish this fully people need to be liberated from their daily struggle for economic survival. Public monies should be exploited for the public good.

All of this requires governance which adheres to international best practice standards.

The republic Sinn Féin wants to build requires an accessible and responsive democracy, recognising and upholding basic human, civil and political rights. It would vindicate equal rights and promote social equality. It would promote economic equality through the exercise of social and economic rights. It would accept that these rights are not only indivisible, but in the interests of all. Citizens should be given maximum opportunity to participate in public life and to stand for public office at local and national level. It is essential for this purpose that public participation in politics is not monopolised by a small number of elected people who see politics as a career.

For that we need a strong emphasis on civic education in our schools and a well-endowed structure of adult education, sport, and recreational and cultural facilities. This republic would introduce imaginative citizens' award schemes and forms of public recognition for people who are caring for the elderly, sick, lonely or dependent or who improve the physical environment, and who render useful public service of all kinds.

Public policy would encourage the voluntary activity of citizens in every desirable area of social life. In its social policy, the new Ireland would support families with children by means of housing, childcare and income support measures, and would encourage mothers and fathers to play the fullest part in the upbringing of the next generation through maternity and paternity leave arrangements, guaranteed return to paid employment and the like. It would give special support to single-parent families to help them meet their particular needs.

Society would develop structures for citizens' participation. Most young people nowadays learn little or nothing of our country's history. They do not know of the people in the past, admirable people from their country and other countries whom they should remember and be proud of and be encouraged to model themselves on. Without knowing this story of the politics of the past people cannot understand how the politics of the present have come about. Irish history is marginal in the school curriculum in the north. In the south, only one-third of school leavers now take history in their leaving cert. Thus the new generation is severed from previous generations, which contributes to making them rootless in the face of the pressures of the modern world. Awareness of progressive traditions can give moral support in life.

Perhaps the most important single public policy decision for society is the content of the school curriculum. This would include knowledge of their country's history, literature, art, heritage, folk music and national games. Teachers would be valued highly, for alongside parents they do one of society's most important jobs, forming the next generation of Irish citizens.

Historically, Ireland is a highly centralised society in its political administration, going back to the days when Britain ran the whole island from Dublin. Over recent decades, Dublin has become more dominant still as a result of centralised administration, bad planning or none at all, and population growth. Real powers should be devolved to local communities as regards schools, social care for the elderly and dependent, and improving the physical environment. The strongly democratic character of such societies as Norway, Denmark and Sweden is significantly due to their traditions of strong local government, with a solid basis in local revenue and taxation powers.

Meaningful powers should be given to local urban and rural district councils; to neighbourhood committees concerned with the environment, social care of older citizens and control of anti-social behaviour; and to towns and cities. A mayoral and local council system such as they have in France might be worth adopting in this country to bring more citizens into local political life. The new Ireland would decentralise power to the local and the neighbour-hood to the maximum extent. It would do everything possible to minimise political and administrative centralisation in its domestic social, economic and cultural policy. Its civil and public service would be run in ways that would encourage movement and exchange of experience between the civil service, business, the community and voluntary sector and the universities. The aim would be to overcome bureaucracy and provide a citizen-sensitive, imaginative and efficient public service, with high morale among its members.

Referendums would have a key place in politics, allowing the people themselves to legislate directly. The new republic would permit referendums to be held on the basis of a citizens' initiative, as in Switzerland and many of the states of the USA. A petition supported by a reasonable number of citizens should be able to secure a national referendum on an issue, the outcome of which would have the character of a binding law. There should be fair referendum rules, to ensure that all citizens are well informed on the issues, to give equal coverage to both sides of the argument, and to prevent rich or powerful private interests influencing the result in an unfair fashion.

The new Ireland would adopt the best possible electoral sys-tem for choosing people for public office. No electoral system is perfect; each has its pros and cons. Basic democracy demands that a fair electoral system would be a proportional one, so that rep-resentation corresponds with the proportion of votes cast for each party or policy option.

A republic of free and politically educated citizens requires a free press and a thriving press and broadcast media. Public policy would act firmly against private media monopolies. Diversity in the media, entertainment and cultural provision should be encouraged by public policy to the maximum, particularly at local level, with the use of subsidies and regulation as appropriate.

The new Ireland would ensure that economic growth takes

place in an environmentally sustainable way and in a manner which enables the state to reverse the erosion of our environment, and bring about a reduction in the output of emissions at a minimum in line with the Kyoto Protocol on global warming.

A single all-Ireland state makes economic sense. Its economic policy would take all practical steps to encourage indigenous enterprise and investment. It would welcome foreign capital while ensuring that foreign economic and financial interests did not become too powerful an influence on national economic policy. It would uphold worker and trade union rights and ensure decent standards of working conditions and pensions for all its citizens. It would act to prevent or control private monopolies and in areas of public provision would ensure high standards by means of strict inspection systems, systematic public complaints procedures and the establishment of administrative tribunals, ombudsmen and complaints commissioners. It would take steps to ensure that land was used productively, particularly in urban areas where huge capital gains are often made by the owners of land by virtue of accident of situation, with minimal personal investment, and where land needed for development can lie unused for long periods, to the detriment of people needing land for housing.

The new Ireland would establish its own currency for the whole island of Ireland, and with that would come the ability to control the rate of interest and currency exchange rate. These are essential instruments of the economic policy of any state that seeks to advance the welfare of its citizens. A national currency is the central economic pillar of an independent state. The new republic would ensure that as regards control of credit, it would advance the welfare of the people as a whole and support the broad objectives of democratically decided public policy. We would also take counsel from those United Nations Conventions, which set out the global consensus on minimum standards for all humanity – including the Universal Declaration of Human Rights, the International Covenant on Civil and Political Rights, the International Covenant on Economic, Social and Cultural Rights, the International Convention on the Elimination of Discrimination Against Women, the International Convention on the Elimination of All Forms of Racial Discrimination and the International Convention on the Rights of the Child.

These are all valuable instruments for the achievement of a fully inclusive society, imposing obligations that all signatories – including Ireland – would meet. They are not merely a "feel-good" public relations exercise. At a minimum, a fully inclusive republic would incorporate the conventions into domestic law so that Irish people can derive the greatest benefit from them. But we should also go further. We should actively infuse all areas of policy and public service with a human rights ethos. All public policy and law should be vetted to ensure that it promotes equality and human rights and fights poverty. This means asking the question of every proposal: does it include or does it exclude? It means monitoring all outcomes and making adjustments where required. It means establishing a system for the effective enforcement of rights. International human rights standards should be expressed legislatively and constitutionally in a fully enforceable charter of rights for all. Sinn Féin campaigned for such a charter, and we successfully negotiated provision for it in the Good Friday Agreement.

The new republic would promote a culture of inclusiveness and equality. It would establish the right to benefit from affirmative action to improve the condition of all those who have faced systematic discrimination. It would also constitutionally guarantee social and economic equality. In this way, it would break new ground.

The fact is that you are more likely to be poor if you are a nationalist in the north, an immigrant or traveller, a person with a disability, a child, an older person or a woman. Hate crime is on the rise, targeting people on the basis of religion, ethnicity, sexual orientation or disability. Children are still vulnerable to abuse. Older people are still vulnerable to neglect. Domestic and sexual violence against women are pervasive social cancers. If the conflict in the north has taught us anything, it is that no one should be reduced to second-class citizenship – on any grounds. Diversity is a strength, not a weakness in our social fabric. We cannot have a fully inclusive republic without respect for diversity and the achievement of social equality by those groups that have been excluded.

The republic of the new Ireland would be secular and anti-sectarian. It would guarantee equality for all cultural traditions. That means parity of esteem for Catholic and Protestant, Muslim and Jew, those of other faiths and none, traveller or settled, national or non-national, Irish speakers and English speakers or those with other first languages. The republic would adopt anti-racism and interculturalism as guiding social values. Its immigration policy would therefore be positive, compassionate, human rights compliant and anti-racist. It would return to a more classical democratic concept of "citizenship" – one that is inclusive of all who reside on the island, regardless of nationality or ethnicity.

The reality is that something exciting is happening in Ireland today. Ireland is no longer just a country of Catholic, Protestant and Dissenter; of native Irish, planters, and an occupying colonial power; of traveller and settled people. Ireland is now home to people from every region of the world. We have become a country to which people immigrate – as opposed to a country from which Irish nationals emigrate – in search of a better life. This new cultural diversification has huge potential to change our national dynamic for the better. It means that not only do we have the opportunity to enrich the cultural life of our nation, but we also have the opportunity to harness the economic engine of immigration as so many other successful economies have done.

It is not all good news, however. A new bigotry has emerged in the form of racism against ethnic minorities. Racism is not new, but it has intensified since Ireland became a "new destination" for migrants in the 1990s and immigration increased the ethnic minority populations on the island. Racism has manifested as official discrimination in public policy against national minority ethnic groups, like travellers and non-nationals, including migrant workers, other immigrants, refugees and asylum seekers. It has also manifested itself in racial abuse, threatening behaviour, incitement to hatred, harassment, property damage, assault and even racist killings. Racist violence is a problem north and south, as it is across Europe. The use of racism for party political gain is also a serious problem.

The fact is that immigrants are an economic benefit to Ireland. Immigrant-driven economies are dynamic. Immigrants tend to be young, entrepreneurial and economically productive. Our own experience of migration and the incredible productivity of the Irish abroad shows us the truth of this. Immigrants do not drain scarce public resources; they generally make a net contribution to the public purse. Quite aside from the economic arguments, republicans oppose racism in principle. We also know what it is like to be on the receiving end of discrimination and violent bigotry. Nationalists in the Six Counties continue to experience bigotry from the unionist and British Establishment. Many people from our island were confronted with anti-Irish racism when they migrated in search of work or a better life in Britain or Scotland, the USA or Canada or Australia.

Irish republicans are committed, therefore, to not only eliminating anti-Irish racism, but to ensuring that we are never complicit in treating others as we were treated. Our struggle for equality applies not just to ourselves but to everyone. Irish republicans are absolutely unequivocal about rejecting racism. Respect for diversity, inclusion and equality are all integral to republicanism and necessary for national unity. Bigotry, cultural supremacy and racial nationalism are divisive and antagonistic to republicanism.

Fighting racism and promoting interculturalism is the responsibility of all of us, but there is an extra onus on public representatives and political leaderships. The new Ireland would ensure that anti-racist education is introduced at all levels. It would repeal all laws that either directly or indirectly discriminate against non-nationals and other ethnic minorities, would provide stronger hate-crime laws and would establish traveller-settled reconciliation processes to reduce localised community conflict and find just solutions.

A national anti-racism action plan is pivotal. This would require all-Ireland anti-racist initiatives, including legal harmonisation. Our laws should be based on international best practice. Thousands of families in Ireland have relatives who are illegal immigrants in other countries. We don't stigmatise them as criminals. We don't call for their immediate arrest and deportation back to Ireland. Instead, we call for sympathetic treatment and regularisation. Others should be afforded the same treatment here.

Our commitment to diversity is why Sinn Féin was the first party to call for the decriminalisation of homosexuality and for having a formal policy on lesbian, gay and bisexual equality. The new Ireland would guarantee equality for lesbian, gay, bisexual and transgendered people. Instead of shame, persecution or discrimination on the basis of sexuality or gender identity, everyone would have the freedom to love and to express his or her true identity. No one should face discrimination or disrespect because they are married, unmarried, in a civil partnership, separated, divorced, remarried or widowed, or because they are either parents or childless. Same-sex marriages and civil partnerships and families in all their diversity would be accorded equal respect in society and before the law.

The new republic would enable people with disabilities to reach their true potential and to live with dignity. It would guarantee needs-based, rights-based access to appropriate and coordinated services, advocacy and support for independent living. It would also guarantee equal access to education and training, accessible workplaces, transport, businesses and services as a result of universal design standards. People with disabilities will then find themselves at the centre, not at the margins of society, and we can all benefit from their contributions.

Cherishing children would be a priority. All children would have equal access to the highest quality free education as of right, as well as other supports necessary to their development into well-adjusted adults. Older citizens would be included and encouraged to participate actively in their communities to the best of their ability, and those communities would take care to ensure that the aged do not live in isolation or die alone. Healthcare – including preventive healthcare – is a right. Instead of forcing people to go without, or to choose between paying rent or doctor's bills, instead of forcing parents to forego medical attention in order to afford care for their children, healthcare would be accessible on the basis of need and delivered to best-practice standards. No more patients languishing on hospital trolleys in corridors or on waiting lists months or years long. All people would have access to the same standard of care regardless of income, but pay their fair share for the healthcare system through direct progressive taxation.

Everyone should benefit from the equal right to education in a safe environment that conforms with the highest international standards. Citizens have the right to be protected from incinerators and superdumps and the siting of mobile phone masts near schools and hospitals. Responsible waste management is a must. This will require efficient management of natural resources and industrial development, as well as environmental protection from pollution and reclamation. That means the development of an environmentally friendly, comprehensive, island-wide, fully accessible public transportation network. It means paying serious attention to the development of non-fossil, non-nuclear, affordable and accessible renewable energy alternatives. It means that all law and policy, including development planning at all levels, would be screened for detrimental environmental effects. It also requires significant incentives for environmental friendly and sustainable innovation, by business, agriculture or the Irish fishing industry.

Equality is good for society – any society. Unequal societies squander the resources of economically excluded groups who, by necessity, develop obsessions with survival, on the one hand, or consumption and escapism on the other. This drains economic and other resources that could otherwise be made available for the social good.

Equality makes sense. Inequality costs society more. The elimination of inequality is not only possible, it is critically important, not least because it allows for the full mobilisation of the available creative human resources. Equality can immeasurably enrich the nation. Investment in equality is actually "good value for money". The good news is that inequality is not a permanent or immovable state. As the 1916 Proclamation recognised, inequality is actually the product of the political, economic and social structures imposed by successive generations of those in power, and these can be changed through ingenuity, cooperation and especially political will. For example, a person who cannot walk is not unequal because he or she uses a wheelchair, but because most buildings (including workplaces and schools) and transportation are designed in a way that excludes people who use wheelchairs. It takes only a few adjustments to allow for universal access. This principle applies more broadly. We are not inherently unequal, in that it is not our characteristics that make us so – inherited exclusive social and other structures make us unequal. We can choose either to perpetuate and reinforce these structures, or to change them to make them more inclusive. Just as inequality is socially constructed, it can also be dismantled.

As a consequence, building an equal society is possible because it is a matter of public choice. We can understand the real economics of inequality and decide to do things differently, to the greater benefit of all.

That is our goal. An Ireland built on positive change, on equality, on partnership. An Ireland which is open, transparent and accountable – a people-centred republic – owned by and responsible to the people. An Ireland in which there is no more war, no more conflict. An Ireland in which the words of hate are silent for ever. An Ireland free of division, injustice and fear. An Ireland where the wealth is invested creatively and more fairly and where our children wake up in homes that are warm. An Ireland in which our schools are properly resourced and where no one waits for a hospital bed, a home or a job.

The resources exist to build this republic – the new Ireland. What is needed is political will and vision.

Republicans can look back over the last few years with some degree of satisfaction. We have, along with others, been key architects of the peace process. We have increased our political strength on both sides of the border. But we still have a long way to go. If we are truly to establish alternative politics to the Establishment parties, then we need to surpass them, not just in our commitment but by our determination to convince others of our relevance, and by our ability to shape a better future for all the people of this island.

But I do not suggest that Sinn Féin can bring about all the changes in Irish politics and society that are required on our own. We should aim to unite all progressive members and supporters of all parties around the basic policies for achieving the republic. We should seek to build an alliance for the new Ireland – one which is free of corruption and characterised by civic virtue and social justice. We should be guided by Wolfe Tone's motto, which remains perennially relevant, to seek to unite politically all patriotic people "under the common name of Irishman", which of course includes Irishwomen as well.

Chapter 4

SINN FÉIN AND THE NATION

The development of Sinn Féin and the constitutional, political, social, economic and cultural history of Ireland are intertwined. At the peak of its support, in the period 1918 to 1922, Sinn Féin *was* Irish nationalism. When it first became commonly used as the national flag, the tricolour of green, white and orange was known as the Sinn Féin flag. This was the extent of national unity under the banner of the movement that swept the country in the wake of the 1916 Rising.

In later years, Sinn Féiners did not set much store by the founding of the organisation by Arthur Griffith. His support for the Treaty could neither be forgiven nor forgotten. His notion of a dual monarchy was anathema to republicans. He had sided with the employers against Larkin and Connolly during the Great Lockout of 1913. He was the man who labelled that sincere patriot and republican martyr, Erskine Childers, as a "damned Englishman".

However, Griffith deserves credit for founding Sinn Féin. His big contribution was to start a national debate about how Irish freedom could be achieved without dependence on the machinations of British political parties in Westminster. Griffith had been a young supporter of Parnell and saw how the Irish Parliamentary Party had become so dependent on the good will of Liberal Prime Minister William Gladstone that they were prepared to sacrifice their own leader. They ditched Parnell when Gladstone and his Liberal Party demanded it.

Self-reliance, independence in the true sense, was the essence of the organisation founded, and the idea promulgated, in 1905. A simpler, yet more descriptive name than Sinn Féin – Ourselves – could not have been chosen. Griffith said in his speech at the founding of Sinn Féin on 28 November 1905: "The craven policy that has rotted our nation has been the policy of justifying our existence in our enemy's eyes. Our misfortunes are manifold but we are still men and women of a common family, and we owe no nation an apology for living in accordance with the laws of our being."

During its first twelve years, Sinn Féin was not a republican organisation, although many republicans were in it. What it lacked in ideological clarity, it made up for in enthusiasm and youth. At this time, the Irish-Ireland movement was flourishing, and Sinn Féin was its political expression. There was a deepening sense of national identity based on the movement to save the Irish language from extinction. Like many colonised people around the world, the Irish were struggling to reclaim our identity. We were realising the sense of inferiority that our status as a colony had created in us. If freedom was to be achieved, it was essential to restore national pride and self-respect.

Conradh na Gaeilge and Cumann Lúthchleas Gael (the GAA) were popular cultural and sporting organisations. The Irish literary revival was a feature of the same period – its chief expression being the Abbey Theatre and the works of W.B. Yeats, John M. Synge and many others. New literature was being written in the Irish language. The cooperative movement and the trade union movement were growing, and the movement for women's rights was slowly emerging.

However, women have since been written out of the history of this period and out of Irish history generally. The following, though of a slightly different time, gives an example of this with a personal twist. The box opposite appeared in the *Irish News* a few years ago. It tells of the public funeral of my Grandfather Hannaway's first wife Alice in 1924.

Our family were very pleased to read this acknowledgement of

On This Day / June 29th 1924

FUNERAL OF FALLS TRADE UNIONIST

THE FUNERAL of the late Mrs A. Hannaway took place on Wednesday from her residence, 14 Inkerman Street, to Milltown Cemetery. Deceased was a well-known worker in the trade union movement and took an active part in the organising of factory workers.

She was connected with the Workers' Union since 1912 and was one of the founders of the Castlewellan branch of that organisation. She leaves four young children and husband (W.D. Hannaway, secretary of the Vintners' and Grocers' Assistants' Union, Belfast Branch) to mourn her loss. The cortege was of large dimension. Representatives from different branches of the Workers' Union were in attendance and wreaths were sent from the General Secretary and General President of the Vintners' and Grocers' Assistants' Union.

---

the role of this obviously progressive woman. My generation knew of Grandfather Hannaway's trade union work, but little about Alice's. I was surprised, however, and moved when I mentioned the above article to my Aunt Kathleen, then a woman in her mid-eighties. She looked at me and said with some anger and considerable hurt, "Why wasn't I told about my mother? Why didn't I know she was a leader?"

Why indeed? Republican women were indispensably involved in many of the emerging organisations and bodies which were giving voice to the sense of renewal and rebirth that was evident in Irish society at that time. In 1900, Maud Gonne and others established Inghinidhe na hÉireann, which began publishing its own paper – *Bean na hÉireann* – eight years later. The paper's motto was "Freedom for our nation and the complete removal of all disabilities to our sex". It was women like Helena Molony who helped set up the trade union movement and the cooperative movement, which helped the development of working conditions within Irish industries and agriculture.

All of this healthy growth, though, was happening in a poisoned climate. Ireland's population was still declining, as it had been every year since the Great Hunger. Emigration was on a massive scale. Outside north-east Ulster, there was little industry to provide employment and develop the economy. Poverty was endemic in the cities. Working people in Dublin endured slum conditions and infant mortality rates unparalleled in western Europe. The working poor in Belfast provided factory fodder, with women and children slaving in mills surrounded by redbrick warrens of tiny, over-crowded houses.

In the countryside, the landless poor lived on the edge of survival while smallholders struggled. Young men and women from the west went to other parts of Ireland, to Scotland and to England for seasonal work. Many suffered the indignity of being chosen by employers like cattle at hiring fairs. Under the Poor Law, people who could not be maintained by themselves or their families were consigned to bleak workhouses. And the Irish-speaking districts were the poorest.

Dublin Castle presided over all this. The seat of British rule in Ireland – as Stormont Castle is the seat in the Six Counties today – Dublin Castle saw a succession of English ministers come and go as they administered this island for the British Empire. When Sinn Féin was founded, the Empire circled the globe and was at the height of its economic and military power. Little did the occupants of the Castle suspect that the meeting in the Rotunda on 28 November 1905 was one of the many little fires being lit all over their Empire that would eventually lead to its total collapse. And in this, too, women played a pivotal role. Some of the women present that evening would become household names over the next twenty-five years, women such as Maud Gonne and Constance Markievicz.

But within a few years of its foundation, it seemed that Sinn Féin would vanish long before there appeared even the slightest threat to the Empire. The return to power of the Liberals in England and their dependence on John Redmond's Irish Party for votes in Westminster signalled a revival of hopes for Home Rule. It seemed that Parnell's dream was about to be fulfilled. An Irish parliament would sit in College Green. Nationalists of all shades, as well as trade unionists and socialists, began to prepare for a new battle-ground – an Irish legislature which many hoped could be developed into real independence and sovereignty.

As late as 1912, Pádraig Pearse was speaking on a Home Rule platform with John Redmond. But once again the machinations of British politics were to change all that. An alliance was forged between the Tory Party in England and the Ulster Unionist Council, which had been founded in the same year as Sinn Féin. Their purpose was to thwart Home Rule altogether. Failing that, they would exclude Ulster, or the six most unionist counties, from its operation. This Tory-unionist alliance, which used force and the threat of force with impunity, was allowed by the Liberal government to dictate the pace of events. Home Rule was diluted. The principle of "exclusion" – in other words partition – was accepted. Fatally dependent on his alliance with the Liberals, Redmond could only meekly protest. This was the single most radicalising event for nationalists before 1916. Pádraig Pearse joined the Irish Republican Brotherhood, and young men flooded into Óglaigh na hÉireann (the Irish Volunteers) when it was set up in 1913. The prejudices of Irish society were evident when women who wanted to join the Volunteers were told that their role would be to make flags and bandages and raise money. Those who joined were denied positions on the Volunteer Executive, and that organisation refused to take up a position on the right of women to vote for fear of splitting the Volunteers. A compromise was reached with the setting up a year later of Cumann na mBan.

Markievicz and others decided instead to join Connolly's Irish Citizen Army. It treated its women members as equals and supported the right of women to the vote. In the run-up to the Easter Rising, women in the Citizen Army played a full and equal part and during the Rising fought alongside the men.

While James Connolly agreed with the cultural and nationalist outlook of early Sinn Féin, he criticised the economic policy of Griffith and his associates. Connolly disagreed with a doctrine that "appeals only to those who measure a nation's prosperity by the volume of wealth produced in a country, instead of by the distribution of that wealth amongst the inhabitants". His criticism was borne out when Griffith sided with the employers during the 1913

Lockout. But many other nationalists and republicans supported Jim Larkin and James Connolly, including Pearse, Thomas Ashe and Eamonn Ceannt. The strands of an anti-imperialist movement were coming together.

Some who supported Home Rule hoped that an Irish parliament, subordinate to Westminster, would actually benefit from the spoils of Empire. But people like Terence MacSwiney had a new vision. In *Principles of Freedom* he wrote: "For the Empire as we know it and deal with it is a bad thing in itself, and we must not only get free of it and not again be trapped by it, but must rather give hope and encouragement to every nation fighting the same fight the world over . . ."

Tens of thousands of young Irishmen – Catholics, Protestants and Dissenters – were trapped by the Empire. They were recruited into the British army by John Redmond and by unionist leaders Edward Carson and James Craig. Over 30,000 Irishmen lost their lives in the slaughter of the Western Front and more far-flung places such as Mesopotamia – now Iraq. Republicans have always seen the First World War as an imperialist war. For the unionists, who bore an especially heavy burden of fatalities, the dead of that war hold a special place. All those who died deserve to be remembered. So also do those few brave republicans, nationalists and socialists who campaigned against recruiting.

Republicans of the Fenian tradition like Tom Clarke and Seán Mac Diarmada saw England's difficulty as Ireland's opportunity. Without them there would have been no 1916 Rising. Their separatist strand joined the other strands or "isms" that produced the Proclamation of the Republic and the Rising, fusing to form the core principles of Irish republicanism. Cultural nationalism, anti-imperialism, feminism, socialism, trade unionism were all represented among the small band of revolutionaries who marched out on Easter Monday 1916 to proclaim the republic and to challenge the British Empire. Since that day, Irish republicans have regarded it as our task to put the Proclamation of the Republic into effect. That remains our task.

Did the British government commit a massive tactical mistake, as many believe, by executing the leaders? Certainly the executions contributed to the public reaction against Britain, against the war and against the politically bankrupt Home Rule party. But we often forget what a terrible loss to the Irish freedom struggle were the deaths of people of the calibre of James Connolly and Pádraig Pearse. It is impossible to know how differently the independence struggle would have turned out had such leaders survived to direct it. Their experience would certainly have helped to form a more cohesive leadership. Maire Comerford, an activist of that period, writes in her book *The First Dáil:* "Nobody survived the 1916 Rising to take part in Dáil Éireann who had had any important part in creating the literature of the insurrection, or who understood its motives in depth."

The Rising had set the agenda, and the reorganised Sinn Féin in 1917 committed itself to the Irish republic. But Griffith and others opposed a republican constitution for the party and wanted what they said were more achievable aims. That division within the leadership of the independence movement remained submerged, not least because of the massive endorsement for the avowedly republican manifesto of Sinn Féin at the general election of 1918. The establishment of the First Dáil Éireann is rightly seen as a revolutionary act, and the Democratic Programme set progressive social and economic goals that continue to inspire. But the establishment of the Dáil was also an opportunity, if the British had wanted to avail of it, to come to terms with Irish democracy. The British government chose to suppress the Dáil and Sinn Féin.

That British government was a coalition dominated by the Conservative and Unionist Party and with Liberal Lloyd George as prime minister. The forces that thwarted Home Rule between 1912 and 1914 now shared the reins of power in London. Imperial interests predominated as the British sought to assert themselves after a hugely costly victory over Germany. The result in Ireland was military repression, the 1920 Government of Ireland Act – or the Partition Act as republicans called it – and the establishment of the Orange state in the Six Counties.

Against all of this, a people's struggle was waged in Ireland with an underground Sinn Féin government and IRA flying columns engaging British forces in guerrilla warfare. The British were forced to the negotiating table. It was then that the divisions and lack of cohesion in the republican leadership came to the surface. Political and personality differences emerged. Perhaps it was inevitable in the leadership of a broad front, thrown together after the first rank of leaders had been eliminated in 1916 and catapulted from rebels to national leaders to statesmen negotiating with an Empire in the space of a couple of years.

The Treaty and the subsequent Civil War were a disaster for Ireland and a success for Imperial policy. We are living with the legacy – partition, institutionalised sectarianism, two states in our divided nation and British jurisdiction still intact in the Six Counties. The role of the British government in pushing the Free State government into Civil War is often forgotten. It was an ideal arrangement for Britain. To paraphrase Liam Mellows, they could now use British arguments in Irish mouths – and have British guns fired by Irish hands on other Irish people in the Four Courts, the opening salvo of the Civil War.

Where I come from, the Orange state had been inaugurated with pogroms against Catholics, running sectarian street battles and the incorporation of the paramilitary Ulster Volunteer Force – lock, stock and barrel – into the new Royal Ulster Constabulary. Nationalists and republicans were now non-people in a sectarian state. This was truly the carnival of reaction, north and south, that James Connolly had so wisely predicted would happen if partition were imposed.

The story of republicanism from 1923 until 1969 is the story of the fight against that reaction. It is a story of internment camps and jails, prison executions, short-lived political initiatives and splits. It is above all a story of courage and tenacity against great odds, a time when stalwarts kept the republican flame burning.

The departure of de Valera to form Fianna Fáil in 1926 opened the period during which the Sinn Féin organisation was at its lowest ebb. Adhering to an ever stricter interpretation of the abstentionist position, the party was relegated to the sidelines. In contrast, the IRA and Cumann na mBan grew in strength in the late twenties and early thirties. This growth was in parallel with that of Fianna Fáil. Many republicans, including northern republicans, believed that the Fianna Fáil project should be given a fair wind and that Dev could lead on – or be pushed on – to break the connection with the Empire, smash partition and reunite the country. It was not to be, and by 1936 Dev was banning and jailing the very IRA which had helped him to power in 1932.

Republicans sought a clear political direction in vain in the 1930s. Many who were frustrated at the reluctance of the leadership to put the movement's radical social and economic principles into effect departed in 1934 to form the Republican Congress. But this body itself split soon after it began. The field was left open to de Valera, who ensured that republicans occupied ever narrower political ground.

For the majority of people, that decade was a time of severe economic hardship. In Belfast, the Catholic and Protestant unemployed united briefly to demand work and social assistance. The "Outdoor Relief" strike was a sign of hope, but the unity achieved was soon broken. The unionist government, the Orange Order and the employers successfully used the tactic of divide and conquer. Protestant workers were reminded where their interests lay – with the state which would ensure that work, when it was available, would always go to them first.

There has been controversy in recent years about the role of IRA Chief of Staff Seán Russell and his contacts with the Nazi regime in Germany. Russell was a straightforward republican in the Fenian physical force tradition. Like many of his generation, he had little time for "politics and politicians", seeing armed action as the only way to remove Britain from Ireland. He saw himself as seeking aid from the German government in 1939, just as Roger Casement sought aid from the German government in 1914. He was no Nazi, nor was the IRA of the time pro-fascist. The IRA had spent much of the thirties in opposition to attempts to establish a fascist movement in Ireland – the Blueshirts, who were subsumed into the present-day Fine Gael party. Former IRA Volunteers also went to fight fascism in Spain.

Many republicans did not agree with Russell's strategy, particularly after the Second World War started; they believed that the neutrality of the Twenty-Six Counties should not be jeopardised. But for others, especially northern republicans, the war was no time to hold back. To them the Six Counties were occupied by England in the same way that the Germans occupied Belgium or France. This was the time of the most severe coercion of republicans on both sides of the border. Hundreds were interned without trial. Republicans died on hunger strike and were executed by firing squads and by hanging in de Valera's jails. Those who survived that period had their commitment tested in the white heat of the harshest repression. One of them was the late Joe Cahill, whose closest friend, Tom Williams, walked to the scaffold in Crumlin Road Prison on 2 September 1942. Joe carried that moment with him until the day he died.

It was only after the war that many of the facts about the treatment of prisoners and the executions emerged, having been hidden by wartime censorship. The revelation of the role of the de Valera government in particular had a profound effect on republicans, reinforcing their view of the Free State as a partitionist entity.

During this very difficult period, Sinn Féin was kept alive by people of the calibre of Margaret Buckley, party president from 1937 to 1950. A pioneering republican woman, she was a founder member Cumann na mBan, a judge in the republican courts under the First and Second Dáil, and a republican prisoner during the Tan War and the Civil War. She was also a trade unionist and for many years held senior positions in the Irish Women Workers' Union.

From virtual extinction, the republican movement was rebuilt in the late forties and early fifties. In 1955, republican prisoners Tom Mitchell and Phil Clarke were elected as abstentionist Sinn Féin MPs to the Westminster Parliament. Two years later, Ruairí Ó Brádaigh (Roscommon), John Joe McGirl (Sligo-Leitrim), John Joe Rice (South Kerry) and Éanachán Ó hAnluain (Monaghan) were elected as TDs. The IRA's border campaign that commenced in 1957 was conceived as an armed resistance movement with attacks on British barracks and posts in the Six Counties. Its scope was limited, and while it had support among many nationalists, it could not be sustained, and it was officially ended in 1962.

Then began a period of political soul-searching for republicans. It was realised that the electoral interventions in the fifties had shown the potential widespread support for the republican position throughout the country. But where it was harnessed, that support was not sustained and could not be sustained when the focus was almost exclusively on the armed campaign across the border and on republican prisoners. Republicans realised that they must give leadership and representation on social and economic issues as well as on the national question.

The bicentenary of the birth of Wolfe Tone in 1963 was the occasion of debate on republican ideas and strategies. At the same time, there were the first stirrings of what would become the civil rights movement in the north. Attention now turned to highlighting the nuts and bolts of the Orange state – the sectarian discrimination against nationalists in jobs, housing, local government, education and planning. For the first time, the bright lights of television lit up the dark corners of the political slum that was the northern state. It was not a pretty sight, and it was a revelation to many in Britain and, indeed, in other parts of Ireland. Comparisons were made with the plight of African-Americans in the United States. The tactics and strategies of the oppressed minority in the USA influenced the civil rights movement here.

Parallel with the growth of the civil rights movement were efforts by the leadership of the IRA to fast-track the political development of republicanism, as they saw it. Of course, there were people who resented any deeper involvement in what they regarded as party politics, seeing themselves as being "above party politics". But most republicans, myself included, welcomed the broadening of the scope of our work and the campaigning on housing, the rights of rural communities and workers' rights.

The problem was that the leadership attempted, in the space of a few short years, and during the escalating crisis in the north, to overturn the decades-old policy of abstentionism, not only from Leinster House, but from Stormont and Westminster as well.

When the crisis came in Belfast and Derry in August 1969, the IRA was unprepared. Personality as well as ideological and strategic divisions crystallised around this lack of preparedness and what was seen as the unwillingness of the Dublin-based leadership to utilise a potentially insurrectionary situation. The December 1969 split in the IRA and the split in Sinn Féin the following January represented a real setback. The Orange state was collapsing. British troops were being sent to Ireland to brutalise and imprison our people once again. The Irish government of Fianna Fáil Taoiseach Jack Lynch was itself divided and torn between the need to be seen to aid nationalists in the north and their reluctance to confront Britain. They also feared the growth of republicanism in the Twenty-Six Counties, which could politically threaten Fianna Fáil. Because of the split, republicans were not equipped to give the leadership needed in this crisis situation, especially in the Twenty-Six Counties.

The slide into militarisation and conflict in the north accelerated as the British government failed to face up to the challenge of entrenched and intransigent unionism. Instead, unionists were provided with additional means and resources to oppress nationalists, and the core issues of discrimination and inequality in housing, employment and political life were ineffectually dealt with.

In the following twenty-five years, a bloody and vicious low-intensity war was fought. On one side, the British state applied all of the lessons of previous colonial conflicts, including the state-sponsored killing of citizens through their surrogates in the unionist death squads. On the other, the IRA waged a relentless armed campaign in pursuit of independence and unity. More than three and a half thousand people died.

But this was a conflict that would not be won by one side or the other achieving a military victory over its enemy. It required a political solution. In the late 1970s, I annoyed some republicans by spelling this out. It took almost another fifteen years to break down the political barriers sufficiently to allow for the development of a peace process. Governments and political opponents of Irish republicans were fixated on achieving victory – some still are. The Sinn Féin peace strategy began to take shape with the publication of *Scenario for Peace* in 1987 and later with *Towards a Lasting Peace in Ireland* in 1992. Dialogue, much of it private, allowed Sinn

Féin with others to construct a situation in which the IRA leader-ship called a "complete cessation of military operations" on 31 August 1994.

This initiative, despite one break, created the context for the negotiations leading to the Good Friday Agreement. As occurs within peace processes, there have been ups and downs. Change, which is at the core of any such process, is very threatening to some people, particularly those who are comfortable with the *status quo*. Irish republicans realised early on that as activists who want the most change we had to be prepared to take the greater risks. The process has been a very difficult one, but in the course of its development nationalist and republican confidence has grown. The willingness to take risks has been rewarded by the increased strength of the republican position. Partition remains, for the time being anyway, but for unionists and the rest of us, political life in the Six Counties will never be the same again.

Chapter 5

UNIONISM

At around the same time as Sinn Féin was founded in Dublin, a group of unionists – constituency associations, MPs and the Orange Order – met in the Ulster Hall in Belfast to establish the Ulster Unionist Council to fight Home Rule and defend the union.

This was a time of renewal for Irish nationalism. The very modest demand by the Irish Parliamentary Party at Westminster was for limited Home Rule within the British Empire, and expectations were high in Ireland in 1912 that the Home Rule Bill would be passed. But the Orange card was played in the British parliament.

In September 1912, supported by the Conservatives, unionist leader Edward Carson set out the Ulster Covenant: "We do hereby pledge ourselves in solemn covenant throughout this our time of threatened calamity to stand by one another in defending for ourselves and our children our cherished position of equal citizenship in the United Kingdom, and in using all means which may be found necessary to defeat the present conspiracy to set up a Home Rule Parliament in Ireland." The Ulster Volunteer Force was formed from among the signatories of the Covenant, and preparations were made for the landing of 35,000 weapons at Larne.

Despite receiving support in Westminster, as we have seen Home Rule was refused. The British government acted, as always, first and last, in its own interest. The response was the 1916 Rising and the Proclamation of the Irish Republic, and years of war, including civil war. In 1920, a British act of parliament imposed partition, dividing Ireland into two sections – the Twenty-Six and Six Counties. The consent of the Irish people was never sought nor freely given.

Unionism had evolved from the Plantation, when those who were settled in Ireland as a loyalist garrison to look after English interests were given power and sectarian privileges. What partition did was to formalise this by establishing a unionist state for a unionist people. The maintenance of this sectarian state depended primarily on the application of oppression in all its forms – anti-Catholic discrimination by the state in job allocation and housing, the gerrymandering of election boundaries to the political advantage of unionism, a heavily armed paramilitary police force with a heavily armed militia – backed up by a wide range of coercive legislation. For the next fifty years, the British government allowed unionists total control of the management of the Six Counties. Throughout this period, the British Crown was the guarantor of unionist hegemony. Unionism was an integral part of the Conservative and Unionist Party. Partition and British control of the Six Counties was maintained through an alliance of successive British governments – Tory and Labour – and unionism.

Between 1968 and 1972, political events in the Six Counties led to the break-up of the old established political order. In 1972, Britain scrapped the Stormont parliament when it became clear that unionism could no longer politically manage the Six Counties. From then until the Good Friday Agreement in 1998, Britain attempted to stablise the political situation in the Six Counties by drawing pragmatic unionists into an alliance with the Catholic middle class and conceding a Dublin government interest. This new political alliance, while dependent on wider political forces, would still be based within a gerrymandered political system where Britain could rely on the numerical majority of unionists. British military, political and economic interests were to be maintained under new arrangements.

British strategy has been built on a strategic alliance with unionism. Historically there is no dispute about this. Tony Blair has conceded that point to me, but he argues that this relationship had changed. The fundamentals have not changed, I told him. The British state in the north is a unionist state. Its symbols and emblems are unionist, as are its agencies and its management. These are the elements that Mr Blair is depending on to implement his policy on Ireland.

British policy on Ireland is still about upholding the union. While Tony Blair may think he is modernising unionism, creating a new unionism and a new union, his strategy and policy mean that inevitably it is the UUP and latterly the DUP which are allowed to set the pace.

However, unionist allegiance to the British Crown, always deeply conditional, is matched by a deep distrust of the British government, and not without cause. As unionists have frequently pointed out, most emphatically since the signing of the Hillsborough Treaty in 1985, the British government has, where it sees fit, chosen to ignore the wishes of the unionist population.

Because of its rigid and reactionary view of politics, unionism was unable to accommodate this change in political alliances. Until the Good Friday Agreement, unionists sought to destroy any form of political institution that did not reflect their dominance of the Six County political establishment. The peace process and the inclusive negotiations it created forced the British and sections of unionism to rethink their approach. But in trying to come to terms with the Good Friday Agreement, the Ulster Unionists swung widely between support for it to undermining and devaluing it. The DUP made no secret of its desire to destroy the Agreement.

The Good Friday Agreement moved beyond any internal Six County settlement. It is all-Ireland, in form and structure. It is about a new political dispensation on the island of Ireland and a new relationship between Ireland and Britain. It is also about fundamental constitutional and institutional change and a range of cultural, social and economic safeguards for all citizens. In essence, the Good Friday Agreement is about establishing a level playing field. A level playing field – the implementation of an equality agenda – will make it impossible for triumphalism, exclusion and supremacism to flourish. A level playing field undermines the very reason for the existence of the northern state, and for this reason there are unionist politicians who are dogmatically opposed to change and to equality.

Irish republicanism is, at its core, anti-sectarian and seeks to bring together all sections and shades of opinion on the island. Belfast Protestants led the United Irishmen in solidarity with revolutionary France and on a programme of demanding equal citizens' rights for the disenfranchised Catholics of those days. That is a proud history, and we invite and encourage northern unionists to become more aware of it and to celebrate it with us non-unionists. The great Protestant republican George Gilmore used to point out that when the Derry Apprentice Boys shut the gates of the Maiden City against the forces of King James, they were disowning the divine right of kings, which James embodied as hereditary monarch, and making a radical political gesture that pointed to the Protestant republicanism that developed in the north a century later. He used to speculate about whether nationalists and republicans should not honour the memory of the Apprentice Boys too, side-by-side or simultaneously with their Protestant fellow-northerners. It is something we republicans should consider.

Because of the shared centuries of occupation, conflict and open war, nationalists and unionists, historically, have had to define themselves, their cultures and their aspirations in terms of their relationship to Britain. Because of our experience of conflict and division, many republicans rejected Britishness in its entirety, whilst unionists embraced every British symbol and gesture. Our resentment with unionism and its reliance on British armed force to subjugate us led to periodic bloody rebellions, followed by sullen decades of rancorous hostility. Unionism, as a colonising entity, has never once stopped distrusting the entire nationalist population, fearing that, if our respective roles were ever reversed, we would imitate and improve upon their sectarian excesses. We must deal with these fears.

Sinn Féin has been in dialogue with members of the Protestant and unionist community in the Six Counties for many years. This dialogue took on an added intensity and importance with the public emergence of the embryonic peace process in 1993. Our position was that a necessary element of any conflict resolution process was inclusive dialogue based on equality and respect. This required a serious, good faith effort to engage with political opponents. In the short term, our engagement was and continues to be about conflict resolution and building the peace process. This covers many issues, including the need to share political power in the interests of all, equality, national reconciliation, building confidence and dealing with the human legacy of pain and hurt suffered by unionists over the last thirty years of conflict. I have acknowledged this in the past and I do so again. Much hurt was inflicted on all sides and by all sides in the conflict.

Our engagement with unionism takes place at a number of different levels: with the churches and business people, people from the community and voluntary sector and with loyalist representatives, mainstream political parties and their members. This has not been an easy process. For some, such as former UUP leader James Molyneaux, the IRA cessation of 1994 was the "most destabilising" event in the history of the northern state. And the man who replaced him was elected after coat-trailing down the Garvaghy Road with Ian Paisley. David Trimble did not enter into dialogue with republicans easily, and the head of the DUP, Ian Paisley, has yet to hold face-to-face talks with republicans. But progress has been made.

Since the signing of the Good Friday Agreement in 1998, there have been many difficulties and challenges. The unilateral decision of the British government, in breach of the Agreement, to suspend the political institutions in October 2002 made a bad situation worse. Much of our efforts in recent years have been about getting the political institutions restored and the Good Friday Agreement implemented. In April and October 2003, we were involved in lengthy negotiations with the Irish and British governments and the Ulster Unionist Party. These talks involved many hours of direct engagement between Sinn Féin and the leadership of the UUP. However, despite reaching agreement and our receiving David Trimble's word of honour, he reneged, walked away and was supported in doing so by the two governments. This caused major difficulties for republicans, who delivered what had been agreed.

In November 2004, we returned to the talks once again in a serious effort to resolve the deepening crisis. The two governments and the DUP were involved. During these talks, the DUP did move on to the ground of the Good Friday Agreement and progress was made, but ultimately they refused to accept power-sharing with republicans. Eventually they will; that much is certain. The only question is when. The DUP know that the only way they will get into power is if they share power. The only way that Ian Paisley can be first minister is if there is a Sinn Féin deputy first minister.

The formal declaration by the IRA of the end of its armed campaign has brought momentum back into the process. At the time of writing, the DUP is railing against efforts to put the political process back on track. Ian Paisley continues to refuse to talk to Sinn Féin, but even on this issue the ground has moved. Again it is no longer a question of will he talk to us. The question is when.

There are many issues for republicans and unionists to talk about, most particularly the need for accountable political institutions that can deliver positive change. A terrible price is being paid in all of our communities as a result of British Direct Rule. This includes job losses, privatisation, education cuts, falling incomes for those working in agriculture, a failure to produce any strategy to deal with suicide prevention, and much more. The best people to make decisions about the lives of people in the north are people who live here. Beyond these financial considerations is the real cost to communities condemned to live in poverty, communities with no accessible healthcare or childcare and communities which do not feel safe. British ministers representing constituencies in England, Scotland and Wales and with no interest or knowledge about the needs of people in the north of Ireland are flying in and out of Ireland taking decisions with no accountability or responsibility. They are acting in the interests of a London government, not in the interests of people who live in the Six Counties. These unaccountable British ministers are making decisions based on the advice of an unaccountable Civil

Service. In other words, the place is being run by bureaucrats. This lack of democracy undermines the quality of decisions being made. Citizens will be paying for these bad decisions in the economy, infrastructure and agriculture for years to come.

Despite all the problems, the Assembly, the Executive and the all-Ireland bodies were beginning to open up politics. This was acknowledged across the north, with all sections of the community being involved in the decision-making process. Good decisions were being made: for example, scrapping the eleven-plus exam for children, enhancing the health service and building the economy. But the progress that had been made is being undone by a British government with a very different agenda. The British prime minister's attitude to CAP reform and agriculture is just one example. We also had the attitude of a Direct Rule minister towards families and communities trying to deal with suicide prevention who sought to abdicate responsibility for the failure of the Department of Health to deal with this serious problem by blaming the impact of the conflict. While this has obviously played some role, the evidence shows that social deprivation, unemployment, the lack of community resources, the under-funding of mental health services and, above all, the failure to develop a strategic approach to suicide prevention are in fact greater causes of the higher than average levels of suicide in the north, particularly amongst our young people. There have also been savage cuts in education services, with programmes to protect rural schools being thrown out. There is no effective economic strategy. Instead there is a reliance on privatisation, with the likelihood of water charges looming ever closer.

Sinn Féin has lobbied for a significant peace dividend – that is, for substantial financial investment – to be delivered for the north and the border communities which have suffered immensely as a result of partition, conflict and division. A significant peace dividend would allow us all to begin in earnest the task of undoing the damage caused by thirty years of Direct Rule, and indeed fifty years of unionist misrule before that.

These are challenges for unionism and questions they need to answer. How will unionists deliver for unionism? How will they

engage with nationalist Ireland? How will they repair their relationship with people in communities throughout the north who
have borne the brunt of difficulties caused by unionist intransigence
and violence? Change is always difficult, even in our personal lives
– even when it is for the better. When taken in the context of a
conflict, change can be traumatic. And this can be made even more
difficult when there are those, both within sections of unionism
and within the British political and military establishment, who still
want to hold on to the old ways. In my view, that is where the serious threat to the peace process comes from at this time. There are
increasing numbers of unionists and loyalists who recognise that
the social conditions which cause concern in republican and
nationalist communities across this island also exist in loyalist and
unionist communities in the north. There are conditions of serious
and severe social alienation in loyalist areas, which lead to genuine
feelings of isolation. In fact, in many ways the Protestant working
class has been abandoned. Republicans want to see the standard
of living of all sections of the community raised through meaningful employment, and the provision of social amenities, places of
recreation and better housing. Addressing poverty and deprivation
by targeting social need is a universal concept, which should not be
bounded by political allegiance or religious belief. There is little
merit in government's offering financial support to any section as
a short-term sweetener. A prolonged and consistent policy, including proper and meaningful investment, which will remove social
grievances and reduce alienation, is essential.

Irish republicans understand absolutely – from our own experience – what is happening in unionist and loyalist working-class
areas. Irish republicans do not want anyone to go into the space
that nationalists and republicans in the north are vacating. We
want to close that space down. We do not want anyone to be
treated the way we were. The process of change that we are
involved in is about creating the conditions for a new, democratic, pluralist dispensation on the island of Ireland and a new relationship between Ireland and Britain. It is about fundamental
constitutional and institutional change and a range of political, cultural, social and economic safeguards for all citizens.

Irish republicans believe that Irish unity, on the basis of equality, offers the best future for all the people of this island. To Irish republicans, the new Ireland has always meant more than a form of political administration: it must be about democratic rights, social rights, economic rights and cultural rights. For unionists, the new Ireland offers a real hope of stability and influence and prosperity. Within the British system, unionists are fewer than 2 per cent of the population; they cannot hope to have any significant say in the direction of their own affairs. As 20 per cent of a new Ireland, unionists will be able to assert their full rights and entitlements and exercise real political power and influence. The new Ireland must be a shared Ireland, an integrated Ireland, an Ireland of which unionists have equal ownership.

The new Ireland Irish republicans seek is one in which there will be respect for cultural diversity. It will be a place in which there is political, social, economic and cultural equality. This means that Orange marches will continue in a united Ireland, albeit on the basis of respect and cooperation. The new Ireland must be a shared place for the people who live on this island. And as part of this, its agencies, its management, its symbols and emblems have to be inclusive.

There are three interlinked challenges facing those of us who want a united independent Ireland: getting the British government to become persuaders for Irish unity; getting the Irish government to begin preparations for Irish unity, and engaging with Ulster unionism on the type of Ireland we want to create. We need to address the genuine fears and concerns of unionists in a meaningful way. We must be open to listening to unionism about what they believe the union offers citizens. A public debate around these key issues can only be a positive step forward. We need to look at what they mean by their sense of Britishness and be willing to explore and to be open to new concepts. We need to look at ways in which the unionist people can find their place in a new Ireland. This is not to underestimate the commitment which some unionists have to the union. Arguably, regardless of how political conditions may change, some elements of unionism will remain irreconciled to an all-Ireland dispensation. Undoubtedly, in every country in the world, there are people who desire some system other than the one they live in. This is particularly so in societies where there have been changes of system or jurisdiction. It is natural in the wake of such developments that some people will be unsettled, perhaps even for a generation or so.

But notwithstanding all this, the fact is that the role of the two governments remains central to any hope or chance of success in achieving these objectives. They, more than any other participants, can create a climate of confidence. Equally, the governments can also, by their actions or lack of actions, undermine confidence. Sinn Féin is very aware that building confidence is a collective responsibility. It is a natural extension and an intrinsic part of our peace strategy. That is why we supported the Good Friday Agreement and why we stayed with that agreement through all the twists and turns of the process since then.

In any process of transition from a partitioned island with two jurisdictions to a united Ireland with one jurisdiction, the Good Friday Agreement can be a template and a guarantee of the rights of unionists. All the safeguards contained in it will provide protection. All of us have to go beyond our personal feelings on these issues. I believe that it is inevitable that we will do so. Leaders must bend their will to build the peace and to represent their respective constituencies in so doing.

Republicans want a just peace. We are committed to peaceful advance and are convinced that, unless historic new arrangements are made between us and the various representatives of unionism, nothing can change in this country. Unless a new Ireland is the ultimate goal of all the participants, we will have achieved only a permanent recipe for strife, where one section will feel itself victorious, while the other considers itself defeated.

Chapter 6

WOMEN

The centre of my life as a young child was my Granny Adams, or Margaret Begley, as she was known by her maiden name. She had a singular influence on me and seemed to possess a remarkable sense of balance and moderation. She had a great regard for education, an innate sense of dignity and respect for people, and she taught me always to have time for people. My grandmother had experienced two generations of political opposition and knew full well the hardships of struggle. Her husband had been active in the Irish Republican Brotherhood (IRB) and had died young, leaving her to rear a young family. As they grew into adulthood, some of her sons were active in the IRA, and her home and family was subject to raids and harassment for decades. Like many women of her generation, she lived her life with great courage, giving selflessly to those around her and making a great impact on her community. It is a travesty, however, that women such as her have had so many barriers placed in their way and have been prevented from bringing their experience to the national stage where it is so badly needed.

There is no doubt that in the decades since the election of Sinn Féin's Constance Markievicz as the first woman MP in Europe and the world's first woman minister, in the years since my granny was a young woman, the role of women in Irish society has changed dramatically. Women who entered political life at the start of the twentieth century changed the rules and raised expectations, but the promise for all of the Irish people, especially women, of the coming together of the three great strands of the national movement, the women's movement and the labour movement in the Rising and the War of Independence was dissipated by partition and the Civil War.

It was the emergence of the women's liberation movement of the late 1960s and 1970s which demanded equality of opportunity in education, training and jobs for women that began to establish the grounds for access to contraception and women's right to economic independence – without which women will never achieve true equality.

Writing thirteen years ago, former Irish President Mary Robinson said, "We need to re-appraise our view of who and what is valuable in our society . . . We must look with fresh and unprejudiced eyes at the work of women, the views of women, their way of organizing and their interpretation of social priorities. To achieve this, we must, I believe, begin at the beginning and alter our way of thinking."

In the time since this speech, women's access to education and proper healthcare has increased, their participation in the paid labour force has grown, and legislation that promises equal opportunities for women and respect for their human rights has been adopted. Women are at the forefront of community development and in the voluntary sector. There are a growing number of women participating in society as policy makers and leaders.

But despite all of this, nowhere in the world can women claim to have all the same opportunities as men. For me, the participation of women in decision-making is fundamental to the transformation of society as a whole. It is not possible to have properly functioning political institutions if half of the population is largely absent. If we want different ideas and values, if we want political priorities changed, women must be visible in leadership positions.

Government policy and EU directives have sought to ensure equality in law for women in the paid workforce, but the narrow focus of this has ensured that inequality persists. The principle has been established; the practice has not. Women's unpaid, caring role remains unrecognised, undervalued and unmeasured, with these women denied basic entitlements in terms of social insurance and pension rights. Eighty-five per cent of women receiving child benefit have no other source of income, and 57 per cent of Irish women working full time in the home are totally economically dependent on their partners. The absence of adequate childcare and family friendly provision also makes it difficult for many women to access full-time employment or to achieve career progression.

Women aged twenty-five and over, and particularly those aged thirty-five or over, face a much higher risk of being poorly paid than men of the same age. All of this creates huge economic insecurity and a complete lack of economic independence. "Nowhere to go" is cited as the most frequent reason by women for not leaving violent or abusive relationships. The sad fact is that one in every four women raising children or managing households on their own will experience poverty despite our economic boom.

Irish women are still disproportionately concentrated in low-skill, low-paid and part-time employment. Older women are more likely to live in social isolation, and one-quarter of women experience domestic violence.

The disadvantages suffered by women are not confined to the less well off. There has been an enormous change in the pattern of women's employment over the last three decades. However, even though women have increased their participation rates and their educational achievements, this has not been reflected in women being represented at the higher levels of management. Since its genesis in the 1970s, the term "glass ceiling" has come to symbolise the invisible barriers blocking women from rising to the top of management. This needs to be addressed, and I support the National Women's Council of Ireland's call for state and public bodies to implement 60/40 gender quotas on boards of management and in the policy-making arena.

Inequalities faced by all women in Ireland are magnified for women with disabilities. They are more likely to suffer income inequalities and have even less access to education and employment.

They are regularly denied access to public services, including appropriate health services. They are more likely to experience some form of abuse, and they experience all the same gender-based obstacles to independence and more.

Traveller women face higher poverty, mortality and unemployment levels, and lower levels of educational attainment than their settled counterparts. They face daily discrimination from the settled community, and such discrimination is still considered socially acceptable by many. In recent times, publicans have attempted to introduce blanket bans against travellers. Settled residents groups regularly organise and lobby to prevent the establishment of official halting sites near by.

The question is, how do you change all of this? I believe that it has to be addressed at a number of different levels: increasing the representation of women in all areas of life but particularly in leadership roles and policy-making, fundamentally changing political priorities and tackling head-on prejudice, stereotyping and discrimination.

Sinn Féin has to start by getting our own house in order. Our commitment has to be to equality and social inclusion. We have to continue to change our party, we have to reach out to those with whom we have so much in common, and we have to bring about the type of far-reaching change which is urgently needed.

Within our party structures, we have pursued affirmative action and gender targets. On our Ard Chomhairle, 50 per cent of those members elected at the Ard Fheis must be women, and a minimum of one-third of regional representatives to the body must be women. We have also adopted a target of a minimum of 30 per cent of women election candidates. This approach has not been without its difficulties and opponents. There was a wide-ranging debate on this issue, with some comrades arguing that it was little more than tokenism and would actually set back the equality agenda within the party. I believe that affirmative action, combined with a strategy and policies to increase the participation and involvement of women throughout the party, will make a huge difference and in time will change the culture of the party. And it is this type of change that we are committed to delivering.

And while we have a lot more work to do, I believe that this approach is working. Issues that were invisible are now hotly debated, and 30 per cent of the Sinn Féin councillors elected in the 2005 local government elections in the Six Counties are women.

We are trying to determine how long it will take until women will be participating in political systems throughout the country with full equality. To this end, we are bringing forward proposals to ensure that women and men have an equal share in both party and public affairs and trying to set deadlines to achieve this.

I believe equality is the most important word in the Irish republican dictionary. That includes gender equality. We have a lot to do within Sinn Féin to make our party truly representative of Irish society. We have incorporated guidelines and directives to make sure we have more women running for office, but we must increase the number of women candidates campaigning for winnable seats for the upcoming elections. We must also increase our representation of women at all levels within the party and at all levels of political representation.

The party needs to continue with radical and political change to facilitate this. That includes male members moving over in order to empower women comrades. We have listened too long to the old argument of there being no women to take on the roles within the party. It is the duty of every republican to both identify and nurture the gender balance within the party. This means recruiting more women into our ranks and creating an environment within the party where women feel both welcome and safe. It also means that we need structures in place which assist women, particularly mothers, to take on roles of leadership. It is not acceptable for women with family responsibilities to be placed into positions of leadership and then left unsupported by the party when it comes to the practicalities of being both a parent and full-time party activist.

The equality agenda and the objective of building an Ireland of equals must be kept at the centre of our work as republicans. The gains of the Good Friday Agreement in respect of gender equality have to be consolidated. Republicans will work to develop and promote the next generation of protections – from the extension of rights-based disability legislation, and the introduction of gender-proofing, broader equality proofing and human rights proofing in the Twenty-Six Counties, to a relevant bill of rights in the Six Counties, leading to the development of an all-Ireland charter of rights through a participatory democratic process.

I believe Sinn Féin has taken a lead in this through our publication in 2004 of a discussion document entitled "Rights for All". The consultation process on this document is ongoing, and already many women's groups have been approached and have submitted their criteria. I have no doubt that the equality guarantees in the 1916 Proclamation were of international significance in their time. A future all-Ireland charter can be just as significant and just as groundbreaking, particularly because the intention is to update the principles contained in the Proclamation and to make it relevant to modern Ireland.

We will continue to campaign for the recognition of socio-economic rights, and in particular on universal access to housing, healthcare and childcare as basic rights and building blocks for women's equality. We have tabled Sinn Féin legislation proposing a constitutional right to housing and Sinn Féin Dáil motions on universal healthcare and childcare. Most recently, we raised the issue of constitutional protection of socio-economic rights in our party submission to the Oireachtas All-Party Committee on the 1937 Constitution.

I know that we will continue to find ways of engaging more women in the political process and of ensuring that the voices of women are raised and heard in our political life. Our goals of freedom, of justice, of equality and peace will only be realised with the full participation of women. There can be no national liberation without women's liberation.

Chapter 7

REVIVING THE IRISH LANGUAGE

The Irish language has more than two thousand years of unbroken history. Apart from Greek, it has the oldest literature of any living European language. It is the badge of a civilization whose values were vastly different from the one which seeks to subjugate us.

Of course, Irish culture is wider than the Irish language and wider than Gaelic games, music, dance and storytelling. I embrace and enjoy hugely the many and varied dimensions of our culture and other cultures from other places. Irish literature through the medium of English is celebrated internationally. Our poets and writers, from Joyce, Friel, O'Connor, Ó Faoláin, Beckett, Kate O'Brien, Enda O'Brien, Ronan Bennett, Patrick Kavanagh, Seamus Heaney, O'Casey and Shaw, have dazzled us with the magic of their words. Our music stretches from U2, Rory Gallagher, Van Morrison, Enya, to Horslips, Christy Moore, Frances Black, Daniel O'Donnell, Tony McMahon, Seán Ó Riada, Donal Lunny, The Chieftans, Planxty, Damien Dempsey and the Kilfenora Céilí Band.

Add to this the myriad traditions of urban and rural Ireland, of ancient and modern customs, of Protestant, Catholic and other religious tendencies, of the influence of the new Irish – those who have come to our shores from all parts of the globe – and we have some sense of the diversity of our island people. This is great cause for celebration and is as thoroughly Irish as any other aspect of our society. So this chapter is a not an argument about some sense of "pure" Irishness; there is no such thing. It is an argument for the revival of the Irish language.

There is a great joy in being able to speak Irish. My conversational Irish is still quite limited. But I try to learn a little bit every day. Even one word or a phrase. When I first started to try to make public remarks through the medium of Irish, I was ridiculed by many of my detractors. But I persevered. I'm still not proficient, but I get great satisfaction in the number of strangers who speak Irish to me. In my own constituency of West Belfast, which has its own thriving Gaeltacht quarter, it is possible to do business through the medium of Irish in local shops, pubs and other places. Some neighbours' children have never spoken to me except in Irish. Out of all of this there is a sense of belonging.

The purpose of this book is to look forward, but to do so it is necessary to get an understanding of what can be achieved, of what has led us to where we currently are, and where we are attempting to go. As Sinn Féin moves into its second century, Gaelic culture is flourishing. Gaelic sports are thriving, both because of their sheer excitement and local pride, but also because of the community participation from the club level upwards. Other factors, such as televised games, fashions (with an increase in the popularity of sporting clothes, including GAA tops), and the GAA's promoting itself to popularise the sport, means that there is an increase in the level of participation and interest in Gaelic games. In this atmosphere, there is a sense that Gaelic games can only continue to grow and grow. But we do not all expect to play for the county and we are happy in sport to have heroes, so sport remains the classic spectator activity.

While the same can be said of dance and song and music (that is, that the non-musicians and dancers and singers in our midst are generally happy to let someone else entertain us while we enjoy their gift), the same is not true of that other great element of culture: the language.

Language is not a spectator sport. Language requires learning, whether it is done as a child, in school or as an adult. The language constantly faces the legacy of colonialism and the threat posed by the growth of globalisation. The almost complete destruction of the Irish language took place as part of a policy decision by the British to eliminate the Gaelic way of life in their first colony. The belief that "as the tongue speaketh so the heart thinketh" decreed that any social or political discourse in Ireland must be in English. Despite this, elements of the Gaelic way of life persisted in many parts of Ireland up to the nineteenth century in one form or another, but by then the language had become the language of the poor, mainly in rural and marginal regions. In the mid-century, a combination of factors around the Great Hunger and mass emigration and the school system all caused what Seán de Fréine named "the Great Silence", when a generation stopped speaking the language and the next lost the language base from which to pass their knowledge on.

In Ireland after the Great Hunger, it would take almost another fifty years before the academics and intellectuals would begin the revival and before the association between Irish and poverty would be broken down. The revival movement would eventually become the national independence movement. Despite all the promise and potential of the mass movement for independence, uniting cultural activism with political activism, the partition of the country meant further suppression of all things Irish in the north. While Irish would eventually become officially recognised as the first language in the Twenty-Six Counties, the task of revival was devolved to the school system. In spite of the obvious zeal of many teachers, and indeed as we now know the over-zealous approach of a large proportion of these, Irish was not revived. Huge numbers of people of earlier generations talk today in caustic terms of being forced to learn Irish and of the association between Irish and compulsion, and of the perceived waste of years of learning a language that they would never use outside of the school classroom.

Languages die out when fewer new speakers replace those of previous generations. Irish used to be in that category, but today interest in the Irish language is growing and many young people north and south want to speak Irish. The census figures published in 2004 record that there are 1.5 million Irish speakers in the Twenty-Six Counties, an increase on the 1.43 million Irish speakers identified in 1996. The last census in the Six Counties recorded Irish language speakers at 23 per cent in West Belfast and 16 per cent in Derry. The traditional difficulty for many people with Irish is not that it is a hard language to learn but that the state failed utterly to ensure that it was taught well, using the most modern methods and contemporary learning aids.

In the Twenty-Six Counties, despite twelve years of learning, many young adults finish schooling with leaving cert Irish and paradoxically sometimes an inability to carry out a conversation in Irish. The huge investment in terms of money and time by the educators and the students alike seems almost fraudulent. It was at best going through the motions and at worst generating a systematic apathy that Irish will never have any value.

On top of this legacy we now face the threat of globalisation. More and more elements of the culture of this country are being replaced by global corporate identity, where we eat the same food and wear the same clothes, watch the same TV and listen to the same music and follow the same sport as our villages vanish into towns and as the main streets of those towns are eaten up by chain stores with shopfronts that are the same the world over. One bulwark remains: the language.

So where did it all go wrong, and what is to be done about it? Máirtín Ó Cadhain answered that when he said, "Activity has two aspects, one of resistance and the other of positive demands."

The key is to ensure that the language is seen to be a vibrant language which is relevant to our everyday lives. So government support and a grass-roots revival is needed. Throughout Ireland there are initiatives which work, where individuals and communities promote the language in the face of governmental indifference or outright opposition.

A graphic example for me can be found in the north where the political prisoners, particularly in the cages of Long Kesh, created Irish language communities in prison. Because these prisoners had political status, they were permitted Irish language text books. Many benefited from the teaching of Prionsias Mac Airt, Cyril

MacCurtain and others. This is where Bobby Sands became proficient in Irish. Many of these prisoners and others who had been interned continued with their work on the language when they were released. Later when the cages were replaced by the H Blocks of Long Kesh, and when the Irish language became the daily language of most of the protesting prisoners at that time, this had a huge impact on the consciousness, particularly of young working-class nationalists. During the hunger strike of 1981 in which ten prisoners died, Bobby Sands' leadership on the language issue and his death had a huge effect. When prisoners were released from the Blocks, many of them brought the language skills and teaching methods they had learned back into their communities, conducting classes in pubs, clubs, community centres and homes. Throughout the north, stalwart pioneering language activists had campaigned for decades for language rights, including the right to education through Irish. Their efforts were greatly enhanced by the popularisation of the language among the urban working class in the 1980s.

In terms of promoting the language, the greatest success stories in recent times has been the growth of the *Gaelscoileanna*, Irish language schools. There are now *Gaelscoileanna* in every county in Ireland, and increasingly these *Gaelscoileanna* reflect the multicultural mix which modern Ireland has become. There are now over 400 *naionraí*, that is pre-school projects, across the island. And hundreds of *bunscoileanna* or primary schools and *iarbhunscoileanna* or secondary schools.

This development of the *Gaelscoileanna* has been driven by communities and not matched by government resources. Because of the lack of government support, the children of the *Gaelscoileanna* often spend their formative years in schools whose physical conditions leave a lot to be desired. But in these school environments, tolerance, respect for diversity, a love for the language, its vibrancy and versatility and value is taught. Irish language education continues to attract new supporters, but almost universally the gains made for these schools, north and south, have required struggle and persistence.

Government support for education is the entitlement of all

children. It is key to promoting Irish medium education. When Martin McGuinness was minister for education in the north, he eased the entry level for new *bunscoileanna,* lowering the number of pupils required to open new schools and thus clearly recognising that the language had a historical handicap to overcome. He also established Iontaobhas na Gaelscolaíochta, to seed fund new *Gaelscoileanna* to develop to the point where they could gain full departmental recognition and a council for Irish schools, Comhairle na Gaelscolaíochta.

Similar measures need to be replicated in the Twenty-Six Counties where the trend seems to be in the other direction, raising the bar and making it more difficult to open new schools. We also need to ensure that the best practices of teaching second languages are applied in Ireland. For example, all trainee teachers of Irish could spend a year in the Gaeltacht in much the same fashion as teachers of foreign languages such as French or Spanish must spend a year abroad on Erasmus or other EU-based language immersion programmes. Such proposals improve the language skills of the teacher and subsequently the learner.

Another key governmental initiative occurred in 2004 with the enactment of the Official Languages Act in the south with legislation to empower the language, providing it with a much needed economic status. This needs to be speedily put on an all-Ireland basis. Through this act more than 640 groups and bodies are now obliged to deal with Irish speakers through the medium of Irish, and hundreds of new positions have been or are in the process of being created. In the next decade or so, we can expect many businesses to have a dedicated section working through Irish. Banks and other institutions will have to provide services in Irish for their customers. Of course, that means customers demanding the provision of this service, citing the provisions in the Language Act. All of these battles have been won because they were waged by ordinary people, by Irish speakers, but the minister responsible, Éamon Ó Cuív, has made a difference.

The decision in June 2005 by the EU to accord official working language status to the Irish language is very welcome. It was due in no small part to the campaigners, and particularly Stádas na

Gaeilge, for their determination, commitment and perseverance. They are to be congratulated. Irish will now be the twenty-first official language of the EU. The significance of this is far-reaching. All EU legislation will be translated into Irish; at ministerial level facilities will have to be put in place so that Irish can be spoken at meetings, and Irish people seeking employment within the EU system will now be able to put down Irish on their CVs as one of the two official EU languages that are required by applicants. Up to thirty translators will also be employed. And, of course, all of this is impacting positively on the place of the language in the north and bolsters language activists' efforts to ensure that they have the same rights there as activists in Dublin, Cork or Galway.

As previous generations know all too well, it is impossible to separate national liberation from cultural revival. The negotiation for the Good Friday Agreement involved rights and safeguards for cultural expression, including the promotion of the Irish language. These rights and safeguards had been absent from the Six Counties since its formation.

Under the Good Friday Agreement, Foras na Gaeilge was established to promote Irish on an all-island basis. This gave a new impetus to the myriad strands of the language revival. For the first time, key decisions on the future of the language were being made on an all-Ireland basis, freeing Irish speakers in the north from the straitjacket of pro-British decision-makers, and allowing Irish speakers to plan ahead on a strategic, thirty-two county basis. Though the on-again-off-again nature of the Good Friday institutions has hampered the work of Foras, it has now found its feet and is providing leadership to the resurgent Irish-speaking lobby. Sinn Féin representatives on Foras have endeavoured to make it a truly dynamic and representative body, giving voice to the grass roots while also putting pressure on the two governments to live up to their pledges on Irish.

The growing status of the language, as it is increasingly used in business, will be of enormous significance in the developing of a bilingual society. Where will the Irish speakers come from to fill these new positions? Certainly many of them will – and should – be Gaeltacht based. The Gaeltacht areas, under such threat from the English-speaking world, not only deserve to be protected, but since they remain the source of a wealth and tradition of spoken Irish, they need the support of the state in ensuring that the next generation have a source of Irish to be drawn from.

The Gaeltacht is more than the sum of its parts. The Gaeltacht is not merely an area where Irish is spoken. It has traditionally been the area where Irish is passed on in all its richness and expressiveness to the next generation. However, most of the remaining Gaeltacht is in rural areas on the western seaboard and has consequently suffered from the economics of urban development or, more specifically, Dublin-centred development. While the uptake of third-level education is high in Gaeltacht areas, for many young people in the Gaeltacht, third-level education is considered their escape route. They leave to go to college and only a small minority return.

Little has been done to strengthen the economic foundation since the 1920s and 1930s. The result of this has seen the economic situation in the Gaeltacht areas worsen. This is an important and a growing factor in the decline of the language. Economic emigration decimated communities. For some, the preserving of our Gaeltacht areas is of primary importance. For others who are not in those areas, developing the Irish language and culture in the Galltachaí (English-speaking areas) is just as important. In my view, all of these are of equal importance and should be guided, examined and supported in every way possible.

The way forward is through ensuring that the Irish language is retained and strengthened as the spoken language of the Gaeltacht areas, while promoting Irish language programmes and developing Irish language cultural centres in all parts of the country. The government has the responsibility to put in place the architecture to promote and sustain the language. However, it is up to communities to take ownership of the language and to make it living and vibrant.

For example, the city of Galway has sought and received the status of a bilingual city. Shopfront buildings and signs brand their names in Irish while notices inside the shops proclaim that business can be conducted in both "*Gaeilge agus Béarla*". Areas in

Belfast and Derry led the way much earlier than Galway. The people in neighbourhoods in these cities have not waited for any Language Act to deliver the changes in the Six Counties. They have been to the fore in providing the choice of education through Irish for the younger generation and the provision of bilingual street signs. The now annual summer festivals which provide wide-ranging cultural and multicultural events, while debating topical issues, have spread from west Belfast to the Derry Gasyard festival to south Armagh, north Belfast and elsewhere.

So it is now obvious that language decline is reversible. With planning and resources, including language planning and physical planning, the current pressure on the Gaeltacht areas can be overcome and the language promoted throughout Ireland. However, such planning will need to be comprehensive, ongoing and adequately resourced and funded.

Ideas which Sinn Féin has included in our recent Údarás na Gaeltachta election campaign include home-based teaching for non-Irish-speaking parents and language impact studies on all proposed new housing developments. The decision of the planning appeal which ruled in favour of a language requirement in several recent cases shows how important this is. Much discussion is taking place as to where the boundaries of the Gaeltacht should lie. My belief is that the solution to this is not to reduce the Gaeltacht but to increase the range of support mechanisms inside the Gaeltacht. Also, places and communities which are outside the Gaeltacht but which have significant numbers of Irish speakers should be given a special status.

Irish speakers in the north do not have the same linguistic rights that have been successfully fought for and achieved in the rest of the island. One only has to look at the lengthy delay imposed on the transmitter for TG4 to realise how it is a battle a day for Irish speakers. The treatment of the Irish language by the BBC provides another example of the obstacles put in the way of Irish language speakers. There is a huge disparity between the treatment by the BBC of the Irish language and either Welsh or Scottish Gaelic. This is clearly demonstrated by the table below, which sets out the television and radio hours and spend on the three languages for 2003/04 alongside figures for numbers with knowledge of Welsh, Scottish Gaelic and Irish drawn from the 2001 census.

2001 Census: knowledge of Welsh, Scottish Gaelic & Irish					
		BBC Television Service		Radio Service	
			2003/4		
	Number	Hours	Spend	Hours	Spend
Wales	580,000	521	£20.3m	7528	£9m
Scotland	63,444	36	£2.06m	2782	£2.95m
N/E Ireland	167,490	8.24	£0.42m	256	£0.24m

The BBC green paper on its charter review indicates an intention to continue to cater significantly for both the Welsh and Scottish Gaelic languages. However, it makes no mention of the Irish language or its obligations to the Irish language community. Its obligations with regard to linguistic diversity and the European Charter for Regional or Minority Languages do not appear to include increased provision for an Irish language audience. This is a major omission on which Sinn Féin has challenged the BBC. Any BBC charter should include the detail of how it intends to comply with the Council of Europe Charter for Regional and Minority Languages with regard to the Irish language. And it should also include a commitment to cater for the Irish language on a scale similar to its plans to cater for the Welsh language.

A lot can change in a decade, as we can see from our own recent history and from events all around the world. Once we believe in ourselves and in our ability and capacity to overcome difficulties, everything is possible. A host of countries and indigenous nations that were colonised by imperialist countries have learned that it is possible to reverse language decline. Even in a place where only one native speaker remained in an American Indian reservation, through the teaching of that language to the younger generation in that reservation and the planning of further programmes which spread initiatives, bit by bit, the language has not only been preserved but its demise has been reversed.

Imagine the potential for the enhancement of the Irish language if the following was actively acted upon at this time even within the limits imposed by partition: the Official Languages Act; the Language Education Act; legal protection internationally; media – including that wonderful Irish language TV channel TG4, *Foinse, Lá,* RnaG; university courses in language planning; third-level degrees through Irish in every main university which is financed by the taxpayer; economic possibilities of providing jobs, creating niches which can be expanded upon; youth ventures – youth radio and TV channels and newspapers; comics and other publications; music groups; plays and comedy. Raidió na Gaeltachta now broadcasts twenty-four hours a day and can be heard on the net all over the world. Recently, it launched a new service for younger listeners with songs in English permitted, *Anocht FM. Lá* has been published as a daily since April 2002 and now boasts offices in the Donegal Gaeltacht and in west Belfast, ensuring that we now have all the elements of modern media in Irish. The teaching of Irish through the internet to anyone, anywhere is another exciting development, as is the fact that you can also learn to play traditional Irish music on a number of instruments through classes on the net.

I mention all of this not only to commend those involved but also by way of illustrating how issues can be advanced. This is proof positive of the merits of Máirtín Ó Cadhain's assertion that, "Issues should be chosen with care. It is better they should not be exclusively concerned with the language but connected with other matters of public interest." Most of the issues, including the Irish language, that we struggle for cannot and should not wait until we have the new Ireland. We cannot and should not wait for some magic day when all these matters will be sorted out. Our job is to sort them out now.

Chapter 8

EMPOWERING RURAL IRELAND

While my family has lived in Belfast for generations, like most Irish city dwellers it is relatively easy for us to trace our roots to rural Ireland, in my case to counties Down, Leitrim and Donegal. Like many others, my family moved to the city in search of employment and better opportunities. These are patterns that continue up to the present day.

Ireland today has a population of just over five million. Life has improved for many people in recent years, but the fact remains that where you live greatly impacts on your life and that of your family. If you draw a line along the course of the river Bann or the river Shannon, east of that line you will find the centres of political power, greater employment and educational opportunities and increasing population levels. Over 40 per cent of people now live in urban centres. More than one-third of the population in the Twenty-Six Counties live in or close to Dublin.

Along with its many advantages, the urbanisation of Ireland, particularly along the eastern coast, has brought its difficulties, especially in relation to the quality of people's lives. The boom of the Celtic Tiger has meant that although many young people are in well paid jobs, they have to spend long hours in grid-locked traffic travelling in and out to work. Many couples are saddled with huge mortgages. Childcare facilities are practically non-existent in some areas. Bad planning and development has seen the construction, almost overnight, of huge housing complexes, with no effort made to build integrated communities with the necessary services such as schools, childcare or youth facilities.

In rural Ireland, things have also changed dramatically. Agriculture used to be the main Irish industry. Nowadays, while it is less important, at least 13 per cent of our people are still directly involved in farming. This is a very significant figure. The practical effects of the declining numbers of people making their living from the land has been the fall in the populations of rural townlands, villages and towns. This was particularly marked in the 1980s and the early 1990s, when emigration again attained mass proportions. I remember once being told that the entire Leitrim under-21 Connacht championship football team had had to leave Ireland to find work. That story could be replicated right across the country. The official government line at that time was that emigration was a positive thing. I disagreed. Travel is good; compulsory emigration is not.

Government neglect and indifference has ensured that across the country, rural communities are disappearing. Families are leaving the land. Local businesses are closing. Population is declining. Travelling throughout the west of Ireland, including the northwest, it's impossible not to notice that more and more villages have no school, no post office, no Garda station and no young people. The problems facing those in isolated rural communities are increasing. The impact on farming families has been particularly severe.

Of 159,000 farms in the south, only 50,000 are deemed economic, and most of those living on non-economic farms have no other source of income. Six years ago in the north, it was estimated that over half of the 32,000 farms are too small to provide full-time employment. But it is important to remember that the majority of people living in rural communities are not farmers. Two-thirds of those affected by poverty in the south live in rural areas, while in the north it is concentrated west of the Bann and in border areas.

More than thirty-five years after the civil rights movement

launched its campaign to highlight the nature of structural discrimination in housing, voting and jobs, these same issues remain
at the heart of continued inequalities. This is particularly evident
also west of the Bann. An annual report published at the time of
writing by Invest Northern Ireland showed that rather than eliminating such imbalance, patterns of inequality are being replicated.
Incredibly, despite suffering from decades of under-investment and
disadvantage, in 2003–04 the six constituencies west of the Bann
received only 10 per cent of investment, and Invest Northern
Ireland plan to continue this pattern of investment. Sinn Féin's
determination is to reverse this. The fact is that such policies
ensure that more and more young people are leaving rural areas.

The effect of the movement of people from the land has been
to create significant regional imbalances, with a lack of infrastructure, jobs and transport in rural areas and congestion in urban
areas. This issue, like many others, is a question of rights.
Whatever part of the country people live in, they have the right
to accessible healthcare, a decent home, work, education and
other services such as pharmacies, public telephone services and
community police support.

There is a pressing need to formulate a strategy on farming and
the wider issue of rural development. This strategy needs to be
built up and developed by the communities directly affected by
rural under-development. Government policy needs to be rural-
proofed: that is, decisions should be examined before being put
into effect, to ensure that they do not adversely impact on rural
areas and that they actually are to the advantage of rural Ireland.
This means bringing together in a structured way all those depart-
ments and bodies which affect rural areas and trying to ensure
that they work together to promote rural development.

The aim must be to keep the maximum number of people on
the land and to preserve the social fabric of rural life. This can be
achieved by creating the conditions in which rural communities can
rebuild their local economies and everyone has a dignified standard of living, access to proper education, housing and health
resources. This requires the revision and maintenance of roads and
other services. Fair and strategic planning regulations are crucial

for the future sustainability of rural communities, which means genuine consultation between local councils, rural communities, farmers and environmental campaigners to develop new legislation for rural development.

Throughout Ireland, there are communities fighting for survival with little or no aid from central government. These communities have often formed their own new cooperatives, local currency networks in border areas, social enterprise and development projects, organic farming and agri-tourism initiatives and other diversified agricultural businesses. There is a need to promote organic farming. It is commercially viable on a much smaller acreage than current farming. There is a need also to encourage cooperative agricultural and broadleaf forestry projects. Ireland should be a GM-free zone. As well as ensuring the quality of food products sold to Irish consumers, this would also be a major boost to the marketing of Irish food products internationally.

The future of farming is very uncertain, and this has consequences for the future economic shape of our rural communities. Farmers feel very much at the mercy of external forces, be they EU bureaucrats, government officials or the major processors who can apparently cut prices at a whim. Tens of thousands of family farms have gone out of existence over the past thirty years. Many times I have been told that the family farm is a thing of the past.

Supporters of the changes in our agricultural industry will argue that this is because fewer people are needed on the land to meet the existing demand for food, but this is only half the story. It does not take into account the structural elements of Irish farming which make a large sector dependent on the export of live animals. This has been the bedrock of Irish farming for a very long time, and there has been no real effort to build a domestic processing sector that would sell higher value products where the demand exists. Instead, there has been an over-reliance on the export of unprocessed produce that boosts other economies.

Fishing has suffered from a similar failure. It has been estimated that 120 billion euro of fish, at current value, was taken from

Irish waters between 1973 and 2003. Only a small proportion of this was taken by the Irish fleet. This is not only a massive loss to Irish fishing communities, but it also represents a huge loss for the economy of the island. Again, there is little effort to develop follow-on industries. Fish caught and processed is worth far more than fish packed in ice and exported. For the government of an island nation, even one partitioned as we are at this time, not to exploit its fishing stocks for the national good is shameful. For fishermen and women it can be a frustrating task to confront the directives that emanate from Brussels and which threaten to destroy Irish fishing communities. The solution requires political will at government level to ensure that our natural resources are developed to our advantage. This means Irish national interests being asserted against both the European Union and the multinationals.

An issue of controversy at the time of writing involves another natural resource. The refusal of the people of Erris, County Mayo, to allow the Corrib Gas Consortium, led by Shell, to lay a pipeline across their land highlights for me many of the problems facing rural communities. The protesting farmers were joined by many of their neighbours, who were concerned over the impact of the project on the area. Many of them also objected to the terms and conditions under which the consortium had been given the Corrib Gas field by the Irish government. The Shell proposals meant that gas would be piped close to people's homes. There were valid and genuine concerns about the dangerously high pressure in the pipeline. For a number of years, no one had paid much attention to what was going on there. Then as the time came for Shell to begin work on the actual installation of the pipeline itself, four of the farmers and a local supporter were imprisoned under a court injunction.

In the county where the Land League was founded by Michael Davitt, such actions are not popular. It is ridiculous that the Irish government had made a deal under which the Corrib Gas could be piped ashore with practically no benefit to the Irish people. Having initially promised hundreds if not thousands of related jobs, Shell were forced to admit that there would be no more than twenty-seven full-time jobs created. The gas being brought in, our gas, would be sold back to Bord Gáis at full market price. Imagine what an Irish government, if it had its priorities right, could do with this natural resource? Look at Norway, whose economic success has been virtually built on oil and gas. The Norwegian state has both a significant stake in the development of the reserves and it makes the multinationals pay proper royalties and tax. The Norwegians have also utilised that other resource we have in common – its fisheries – in a manner that further highlights the incompetence and neglect of successive Irish governments.

Rural life is, of course, far more complex and rich than the economic pursuits carried out in local communities. Nor can rural communities be solely dependent on traditional economic pursuits, be it farming or fishing. But these will remain central. I believe our farming and fishing industries can play an enhanced role if there is a strategy to concentrate on utilising local processing and markets to the greatest extent.

There can also be a much greater role in employment creation for local indigenous industry. There is, for example, a growing niche for cottage type industries that are often related to farming. The bulk of government funding for economic development currently goes to foreign-export-orientated companies. In my view, there should be equity in the allocation of funding. Indigenous enterprise projects need to be fully supported. Instead of deploying the state's resources to draw everything, and everyone, towards urban centres, they should be utilised to foster local initiative and locally based services.

The republican vision for rural Ireland is inseparable from our vision for a new Ireland that embraces people from all traditions and all parts of Ireland. Many of the values which shape our national character – community, heritage, culture – are drawn from our rural roots. By the same token, many of the worst aspects of modern life – poverty, isolation, prejudice – can be magnified there. All citizens have the right to live free from such difficulties. We have the ability to create the conditions where this can happen and to reverse the regional imbalances which divide our island. Perhaps that vision can be best summarised as wanting to bring the best of rural life into the cities, and the best of the cities into the countryside. And out of that, we hope, will come a more balanced and richer national life.

Chapter 9

A WORLD OF EQUALS

Ireland, as a country that has suffered from colonialism, has a natural affinity with other colonised countries about the globe. Given our history, it is not surprising that we have a world view which is shaped by our experience. It is no accident that Irish people are famously generous in their contributions to victims of famine and our opposition, for example, to the war in Iraq. Of course, not everyone on the island of Ireland supports these positions. But I believe Ireland's foreign policy should be of a progressive kind, in support of struggling people, against the abuse of power and for the development of societies in which everyone is treated on the basis of equality.

This is not to say that Irish people have some special or better position on these issues than people from other nations. Throughout the world, there is a view which wants to see disarmament, an end to poverty and world peace, so we have no monopoly on these issues. However, Irish republicanism has always been firmly internationalist, drawing its inspiration from the revolt against British rule by the American colonies and from the French Revolution. The founders of Irish republicanism, Wolfe Tone and the Society of United Irishmen, saw themselves as citizens of the world and as champions of the cause of freedom in every land. As James Connolly observed in *Labour in Irish History*, the United

Irishmen "understood that the Irish fight for liberty was but a part of the world-wide upward march of the human race".

The Easter Rising sparked an international debate among progressive movements about the use of armed struggle. At a time when Europe was involved in a great conflagration and the Great Powers were fighting for dominance on the Continent, the efforts of those patriots to free Ireland was greeted with trepidation by the ruling classes across Europe. They feared that it could provide an example to subject peoples within the borders of the existing empires. The sighs of relief in the courts and chancelleries of the Great Powers must have been audible when the British brutally suppressed the Rising and executed its leaders. The subsequent Black and Tan War in defence of the republic and in pursuit of national political independence was the continuation of one of the first great anti-colonial struggles. The tactics used by the IRA in that war provided a blueprint for many liberation movements across the world. Even though Ireland has yet to fully succeed with completing its struggle for independence and unification, our historical experience gives us a special affinity with other peoples who have fought for independence and national self-determination.

Irish republicanism has been influenced by many major political movements and ideologies, including political and cultural nationalism, secularism, anti-sectarianism, equality, trade unionism, socialism, anti-colonialism, feminism, civil rights and anti-globalisation campaigns. All of these movements and ideologies are international in their character and have had a lasting impact on Irish republicanism. Republicanism today needs to have a clear view of Ireland's place in the world. Will we surrender decision-making on Irish foreign policy to the big powers, or will we pursue an independent course? Will we deal with the other former colonised nations as equals, or will we join in helping to exploit them as part of one of the world's economic and political power blocs?

The big central international struggle of our time is to assert democratic control by people over the decisions which affect their lives. This does not mean retreating behind existing borders and refusing contact with the outside world, but it does mean reasserting the primacy of democracy and working together in order to pursue this objective.

The world we live in is dominated by the republican struggle, the national struggle, the aspiration of nations to make their own laws and decide their relations with other nations. This is internationalism, not nationalism, of course. The fundamental principle of republican political conduct is internationalism. As internationalists we stand for the emancipation of humankind from all objectionable political bonds imposed from outside. Humankind is divided into nations. We stand for the freedom of humankind. Therefore, we stand for the independence of nations, commencing with our own. This is a broad nationalism, not a narrow kind. Our Irish republicanism is a local expression of our primary internationalism, which makes us friends with the democrats of every other nation.

When the Second World War ended in 1945, there were some fifty-five states in the world. Today there are nearly two hundred, as the old colonial empires have broken up and new nations and states have emerged. The dispute over the partition of Ireland is in part a dispute over what should be the boundary of the Irish and the British states. The British state may yet dissolve into its Scottish, Welsh and English component elements. There are dissatisfied national movements in Catalonia, the Basque country, and among the Bretons, Flemings and other smaller nationalities in western Europe. If there are still unsolved national problems in western Europe, where politics has been concerned with the business of nation state formation for centuries, there is clearly still the potential for other new nation states to be formed in eastern Europe, in addition to those that have come on to the stage of history in recent years.

Since 1989 the USSR has dissolved into fifteen states, Czechoslovakia into two, Yugoslavia into half a dozen, and there are still many more peoples in eastern Europe who aspire to establish a republic of their own. If that is the situation in Europe, the process of nation state formation has scarcely begun in Africa and Asia, where countless millions are gradually coming to a national consciousness as clan and tribal ties based on kinship diminish or disappear in face of modern economic development.

Look at those straight lines on maps that mark the boundaries of most African and Asian States. They were drawn by the rulers of the European empires, the great nineteenth century colonial powers. It was Winston Churchill who drew the boundaries of Iraq, so betraying and locking the Kurds in a political prison. Germany's Bismarck presided over the parcelling out of Africa. The boundaries of most of these former colonial states bear little or no relation to the wishes of their indigenous peoples, who usually speak many different languages and share different cultures. Our new century will certainly see new nation states in Africa, South Asia and the Middle East.

Republicanism will be the political ideology of many of the new states that are in gestation. Perhaps some of them will learn from the Irish experience of nation and state building. Those who say that we are living in a post-nationalist world, and others who assert that the nation state is out of date, should look at the political world around them. Contemporary history shows numerous examples of the working out of the principle of nations exercising their right of self-determination. At the same time, we all form part of the global village: a world where instant communications, the internet, cheap foreign travel, the growth of trade and mass movements of capital and people, and a growing international awareness of global environmental problems and possibly catastrophic climate change, bind humankind ever closer together and make us ever more aware of the common problems we all face.

To tackle these or to solve them we need the free cooperation of free peoples. There can then be cooperation between political equals. This is the negation of all imperialist-type, exploitative relations between states. It is republicanism as applied to international relations.

When the various international institutions were established in the wake of the Second World War, the aim was to improve a dire post-war situation. Even those institutions which we associate with rigid enforcement of the will of international big business began their existence with a progressive mission. The World Bank and the International Monetary Fund were established in order to facilitate post-war reconstruction. Later their remit expanded to promoting the development of post-colonial economies. Their stated role was, originally, to bring about an end to world poverty. Increasingly, however, the prescriptions they offer have the effect of exacerbating poverty, of pushing peoples and nations into a downward spiral of underdevelopment and disempowerment and subordinating these countries' interests to those of the big states, the former imperial powers and such collective blocs as the European Union.

On its own, no nation can successfully stand up to the world financial institutions and their current fundamentalist conservative prescriptions. What is called for is international cooperation among states for real human development. Countries need to work together to make these global financial systems more democratic. This can begin by people putting pressure on their governments to place more importance on the needs of people than the profits of big business.

The United Nations has the potential to be more effective than it currently is, but it requires reform. The major powers have pushed a limited agenda based on big security issues and what they describe as the war against terrorism. They have sidelined the General Assembly of the UN in order to take the real key decisions in the Security Council, where they have a veto. They have actively undermined the efforts of UN and world leaders who have a genuine interest in serving all the world's peoples. They have pushed the whole social and economic agenda of the UN system into the arms of the international financial institutions that are dominated by the richer states (World Bank, International Monetary Fund, World Trade Organisation), where by virtue of their wealth they have a stranglehold on decision-making and can push through policies which benefit the richer countries and further impoverish those countries which are already poor.

The old imperial powers in Europe have never really come to terms with the loss of their empires and have been seeking ways to continue to exploit their former colonies. The international financial institutions give them an instrument to achieve precisely that. Multinational companies rule, using the rhetoric of freedom and democracy. And when nations make genuine cooperative efforts to improve their situation, such as was the intention of the African Union, the richer countries push a programme which makes aid dependent on the adoption of policies of privatisation and the opening up of their markets to unfair competition from the more advanced industrial countries, as well as the multinationals, as for example the New Partnership for Africa's Development (NEPAD).

The principle of equality has been attacked, undermined and rejected on the world stage in recent times. The discourse of consumer choice and competitiveness has taken firm hold even among traditionally left-of-centre parties. There is little principled opposition from "mainstream" social democratic or left-wing parties to the ideological and economic onslaught of the conservative right wing. The idea of "human and civil rights" has become highly qualified, particularly in the social and economic field. This is at a time when rights need to be more than ever vigorously asserted and jealously defended. There are, however, some positive trends in the field of equality. The position of women has improved in many countries, especially in the more developed parts of the world. On the other hand, in the world as a whole, because of massive population growth in the poorest countries, each year probably sees more women worse off than the year before. Racism is far less tolerated than it has been in the past, even though it continues to be a huge problem. But the clearest indicator of growing inequality for vast numbers throughout the world is the gap between rich and poor among the nations. While the rich countries of the west get richer, fifty-four countries in the world saw an average decline in their income per head during the 1990s, a decline which still continues in the 2000s. Within countries, the gap between rich and poor also tends to be growing in all parts of the world.

Privatisation of public services is one of the biggest factors in further impoverishing people. The privatisation of basic services and utilities such as water, education, health, energy and other natural resources puts those things beyond the reach of many, and not only in developing countries.

Equality and democracy are interdependent. If governments are prevented from improving the social and economic situation of their people, what value does democracy hold for those people? Unless governments can assert their role in social and economic development, democracy itself will be discredited and undermined.

This leads us to an issue which increasingly exercises republicans. How will republican ministers operate in government in a world where inequality, exploitation, blackmail, extortion, legalised banditry and resort to force to achieve political and economic objectives are considered the normal form of interaction between nations?

The ANC government in South Africa has been grappling with such issues. In post-apartheid South Africa, the oppressed and disenfranchised majority rightly felt that the decades of social and economic marginalisation they had endured should come to an end with the end of their political exclusion. But the ANC in government has been obliged to make compromises with the forces of international big capital and globalisation and in doing so has disappointed, even if it not yet totally disillusioned, many of its supporters. A similar dynamic has been taking place in Brazil since the election of Lula da Silva to the presidency of that country.

While the experience of larger nations such as South Africa and Brazil, with all of their substantial resources, is important to examine as Irish republicans try to get to grips with these problems, we should not lose sight of the fact that smaller states do have the advantage of being more flexible. It is easier to turn around a small boat than an ocean liner! That is one reason why the richest and most developed states in the world as measured by their average income per head are small ones: e.g. Norway, Switzerland, Finland, Denmark and Singapore.

The need for sovereign states to cooperate with one another is obvious, all the more so when faced with the pressures of globalisation. Fortunately, some important new dynamics of cooperation are developing in the contemporary world. Developing countries that are determined to change the logic of a world economic order, which consigns them to poverty and underdevelopment, have started to come together to defend their interests in world trade talks. Despite being continually lectured about the catastrophic consequences for them if they do not submit to the inevitability of globalisation by opening their markets and services to the privateers, profiteers and asset-strippers of the advanced capitalist countries, they have stood firm and refused to accept trade agreements that are unbalanced and unfair. There are attempts to develop new approaches to cooperation between developing countries which are mutually beneficial and which do not transfer their national wealth to the already rich countries.

Ireland needs to recognise all its friends in the international community and to work with them, rather than allowing itself to be locked into an EU superstate whose policies are dominated by the former west European colonial powers. This does not mean cutting ourselves off from our European and North American links; rather it means using our voice in Europe and North America to help make the world a better place for all of its peoples.

In a global context, redistribution of wealth between nations will involve fair trade and the cancellation of Third World debt. It will mean reorganising the world economy to allow developing countries the freedom to develop socially and economically. It will mean developing countries are able to manage their own resources, with the developed countries paying fair prices for their products, and allowing them to add value to their raw materials themselves by developing their manufacturing and industrial bases, rather than others paying minimum or decreasing prices for those raw materials. A policy of advancing international equality between states means finding ways to effectively regulate multinational corporations and to tax international financial transactions – including the introduction of a Tobin Tax.

Tobin Taxes are simple sales taxes on currency trading across borders. Currently, more than $1.9 trillion dollars is traded each day by banks and currency speculators. Everything that is bought and sold between countries entails currency exchanges, from goods and services to travel to capital investment. (Housing is not traded between countries and therefore does not entail currency exchanges.) Institutions and people buy foreign currency continually to hedge against currency fluctuations. This money trade is more than fifty times the value of all these other markets combined. Even a tiny tax on such international transactions could lift millions of the world's poor out of poverty and provide essential items like clean water, medicines and education.

The original proposal for such an approach came from Dr James Tobin, a Nobel laureate economist at Yale, but his approach has since been refined by others. Tobin proposed that each international trade could have a levy estimated from one-tenth to one-quarter of 1 per cent imposed on it. He estimated that this could raise from $100 billion to $300 billion dollars each year. Tobin Taxes can be enacted domestically by national legislatures, but would require multilateral cooperation to be effectively enforced. In July 2004, Belgian parliamentarians took a historic vote in their Assembly when they passed legislation for a Currency Transaction Tax (CTT), becoming the second European country after France to take such a step. In September 2004, world leaders like Presidents Chirac of France and Lula da Silva of Brazil, Prime Minister Zapatero of Spain and UN Secretary General Kofi Annan pronounced that: "a tax on foreign exchange transactions is technically feasible".

Establishing international equality and justice means allowing countries to invest in essential services such as water, energy, education and health, without putting pressure on them to open up their markets and to privatise such public services. The past decade has seen an increased awareness of the structural nature of global poverty and inequality – the economic policy choices made by richer countries which in some cases have the effect of literally killing millions of people in poor ones. This has given an impulse to encourage the development of new alliances and new forms of cooperation between people in different countries who are working on a broad global justice agenda. Recent years have seen a myriad of local, national and regional forums and initiatives, many of which, despite the posturing of some extremist groups, have become important focal points for grass-roots initiatives and progressive politics.

Regardless of the importance of grass-roots movements, the overall solution of global problems will only be possible within a system of international collective security. This means economic, social and environmental security, as well as security from attack. In this respect, the United Nations has a unique part to play in bringing together all states in the world and providing a forum wherein the common problems facing humankind can be discussed and agreement sought on how to tackle them. International economic and social development can no longer be left to the undemocratic international finance institutions, which have proved themselves incapable of fulfilling their original mission and have instead been serving the interests of the world's most powerful countries.

The cause of international security has to shift from a purely militaristic agenda, which attacks democratic rights and civil liberties in particular countries, to dealing with the real causes of insecurity in the world. For most people, security is about having a decent home or having enough to eat. For the majority of people in the world, insecurity is about not having access to clean drinking water or to medical services. It is about their children dying from treatable illnesses. For many, it is about being prey to arbitrary arrest and detention, and about a lack of access to justice. In some countries, it is about people being targeted for assassination by government because they dare to demand their social, economic, cultural and democratic rights.

The problems of the international security agenda tend to be presented in a very biased way by the economic interests which control the majority of the world's mass media, and which in many cases can decide the fate of governments. The security agenda which sees security as primarily a matter of policing, more effective repression and the promotion of the conservative right wing economic model of the global elites is not going to deliver global security in any meaningful way in the long term. The universal right to freedom from fear of attack and the right to guard against any such threat must also be upheld.

Despite Ireland's historical neutrality, the Irish government has incrementally moved to a position of supporting the security agenda of the world's great powers. This is why we need to adopt a policy of positive neutrality and enshrine it in the Irish

Constitution. We need to ensure that the republic pursues an independent foreign policy. We should not join or form an association with any military alliance, and we should oppose the militarisation of the European Union. We should refuse to condone policies or military groupings which maintain nuclear weapons and any weapons of mass destruction.

The United Nations will need to assert an agenda that reflects the true needs and interests of the peoples of the world. The UN General Assembly and a more open, accountable United Nations has to have more influence in the affairs of the world. The composition of the Security Council will need to be made more democratic. Proper weight must be given to the majority of the world's people who do not find their voice in the current permanent membership of the Security Council.

Another world is possible. How is this to be done? Bono and Bob Geldof and other activists have pointed to a different way. NGOs work away at the coalface. But they can all only do so much. Over one billion people live on less than one dollar a day. Throughout the world, eleven million children under the age of five die each year from preventable diseases. Millions die from malnutrition and such treatable illnesses as measles. The time for the cancellation of the foreign debts of developing countries is long overdue.

After natural disasters, many contributed to by the environmental policies of richer countries, the international media focuses in on the plight of the victims. Some years ago, many thousands of people in Mozambique were drowned by some of the most devastating floods in recent memory, and many tens of thousands more were left homeless. What was not deemed so newsworthy at that time was that while many of the people of Mozambique were clinging to trees and rooftops just to stay alive, their government was being forced to send $1.4 million a week to its debtors in the then G7. At the time Hurricane Mitch hit Central America, Honduras and Nicaragua were spending over half their government revenue on debt repayments. Six years ago, while sixteen million faced starvation in the Horn of Africa, thirty-seven African countries owed a total of 354 billion dollars.

The UN estimated that if the funds to pay off debt were diverted back into health and education, the lives of seven million children a year could be saved. Seven million children! That is two million people more than the entire population of this island. That is 134,000 children a week, dying from preventable diseases. 134,000 children.

Ireland's social and economic problems are but a shadow of the great poverty, inequality and distress experienced by other nations. But they are no less real for our own people who have no jobs, for the elderly, the sick, lone parents, the disabled, for the travelling community and for working-class communities ravaged by the scourge of drugs. All of these wrongs can in principle be righted, especially now that there are the resources in our society to do so. There is still a lot of idealism and compassion and a sense of public service in our society. One of the dangers of the recent scandals and the revelations of abuses which rocked the southern state, and an effect of the affluence of the Celtic Tiger, is that Irish society could be redefined into a less caring and more selfish form of *mé féinism*. That has not happened, but there is a cynicism about politics – and there is a lot of materialism. Of course, people want to be better off. That is natural. But most people also want to help others. We are told that Ireland in these Celtic Tiger times is a less caring place, but the popular response to the victims of disasters elsewhere contradicts this view.

There are many challenges in this increasingly divided world. War in Iraq, conflict in the Middle East, countless wars in Africa, unimaginable poverty and deprivation across the globe, hunger, disease, environmental disasters and the fear of more to come, globalisation and the exploitation of workers, racism and sectarianism, injustice and oppression. The reality of our time is that more money is spent on military projects than on aid or fair trade policies. The reality is that the big powers do not conduct themselves in a globally responsible way. The reality is that there is a crisis in many international or multinational institutions and agencies, like the United Nations. The genocidal consequences of recent events in Rwanda, in the Democratic Republic of the Congo and most recently in Darfur, Sudan, must not be repeated.

These are some of the matters which confront us as Irish republicans engaging with our world. I believe Irish citizens impact on these issues, but only if we make the effort. I believe that another world, a better world, is possible. The response to the tsunami at the beginning of 2005 showed that people, so-called ordinary people, understand the importance of practical as well as symbolic acts of international solidarity. And where the people lead, governments follow.

Chapter 10

SINN FÉIN, EUROPE AND THE EUROPEAN UNION

Three main elements – political, economic and bureaucratic – have gone into making the European Union what it is today. And all of these elements have been backed up by the drive towards militarisation.

France, Germany, Italy, the Netherlands, Luxembourg and Belgium – the key countries that established the original EEC – were all invaded, conquered and occupied during the Second World War. Apart from Luxembourg, these have all been world imperial powers with extensive colonies abroad, especially in Africa. After 1945 they found themselves in a world dominated by the two superpowers, America and Russia. Their ruling elites felt that if they could not be big powers individually any longer, they could be a big power collectively if they united. They could establish a collective neo-colonial empire and maintain relations of trade dominance with their former colonies. France and Germany were confident that if they agreed among themselves, they could have the lead role in running a new integrated western Europe and prevent the other members of the new bloc imposing on them policies they did not want. Britain, which had been one of the victors in the Second World War along with America and Russia, did not join in initially.

After the debacle of the 1956 Suez Crisis brought home to Britain's rulers that she could no longer be a big power on her own, Britain was urged to join the EEC by America, which saw this move as strengthening the economic basis of NATO during the Cold War. Still hankering after its old imperial role, the rulers of Britain hoped either to divide France from Germany inside the EEC or else to be co-opted by them as an equal third partner in running the collective grouping. Thus far Britain has failed in this, and these tensions are still playing themselves out.

The desire to turn the EU into a superpower under the hegemony of the big states, a European superpower that would dispute the world with the US superpower and with other such rising powers as Japan, China and India, is central to understanding the politics of the EU. It is central to the outlook of the key elites involved. And this view can be seen in the arguments of those in Ireland who would say that a strong, federal EU is required as a bulwark against a militarily belligerent US. This, of course, is the polar opposite of the democratic and anti-imperial outlook of Irish republicanism, as well as democrats and progressive people all over Europe.

The EU is not Europe, of course. There are nearly fifty states in Europe, of which twenty-five are in the European Union. Outside the EU are states like Russia, Switzerland and Norway, which are quite as "European" as any EU member. Europe is the geographical name of the continent we live in. For many, the name stands also for our continent's enormous cultural achievements and contributions to human values, science and knowledge. It is perhaps the greatest achievement of the propagandists and spin doctors of the EU integration project that they have been able to collar the word Europe for what is really the EU, just part of the real Europe.

The second element that has gone into making the EU is economics. The EU provides ideal terrain for the west European-based transnational firms. The rules of the EU treaties make free movement of goods, services, capital and labour into principles of supranational EU law that are enforceable by the EU Court of Justice and binding on EU member states and their citizens. These laws prevent the EU member states imposing any controls on capital or from using state aid in ways that would "distort competition with the internal market", irrespective of whether that aid was being used to save jobs or deliver public services to those who cannot afford services provided privately. Not surprisingly, the European-based transnational firms are among the principal lobbyists for further EU integration. They see this as the best way of undermining workers' rights, labour standards and national welfare states that have been struggled for by the labour movements of the different countries over decades.

The EU is unique in the world in that it is a system whereby supposedly sovereign states and their citizens are bound by a continual flow of supranational laws from the EU institutions set above them. This means, of course, that the EU member states are no longer really sovereign or independent. The EU Commission is the only body allowed to propose EU laws, known as directives and regulations. Its commissioners are not elected by citizens but are supranational civil servants who are nominated by EU member governments. The Commission's proposals for new EU laws are then decided on by the twenty-five members of the EU Council of Ministers, of which each country has one minister; therefore, the Council is the prime maker of EU laws. The European Parliament can propose amendments to most, though not all, laws, but it cannot impose such amendments without the agreement of both Council and Commission. Neither can the EU Parliament initiate any laws. The net result is that the twenty-five member Council of Ministers, not the European Parliament, makes laws for 450 million Europeans, and moreover it makes them in secret.

What influence does the Irish government have in making EU laws, which now amount to well over half the new laws we have to obey as citizens each year? (The Six Counties has no commissioner.) The Twenty-Six Counties has one commissioner out of twenty-five. That is 4 per cent representation, but under the Nice Treaty, it will not have any at all from time to time once the EU reaches twenty-seven members, when the number of commissioners will be reduced to fewer than the number of states. On the Council of Ministers, Ireland has one minister, who wields seven out of 237 votes – a qualified majority for making an EU law being 169 votes. That is less than 3 per cent of the total voting weight. In the European Parliament, the Twenty-Six Counties has thirteen seats and the Six Counties three, out of 732 MEPs altogether. That is 2 per cent of the representation.

The third element going to making the EU is what I call the bureaucratic factor. Like all bureaucracies, those who run the EU institutions want more personal power for themselves. The more policy-making is shifted from the twenty-five member states to Brussels, the more power a few hundred politicians, bureaucrats and judges get to make laws and decide things for the 450 million people who belong to the twenty-five-member EU. It is not surprising that few of those running the EU are calling for powers to be returned to the EU member states. At state level, ministers must have a majority in their parliaments to get something done. It is parliaments that make the laws. Ministers are part of the executive arm of government and are subordinate to the legislative arm and separate from the judicial, as part of the classical separation of powers that has long been recognised as fundamental to democratic government. In the EU, however, when powers are shifted from the national to the supranational level, those state ministers are turned into lawmakers for 450 million people on the EU Council of Ministers. Their own personal power increases greatly thereby at the expense of their parliaments and fellow citizens.

Meanwhile, the parliaments and citizens of Ireland and the other EU member states find that they decide less and less. They find their independence and democracy fundamentally eroded and their traditional institutions of state decision-making hollowed out. They find that power has passed gradually from the national to the supranational level, where they have no control and very little influence. Not surprisingly, they have become massively disillusioned, and this disillusion is now growing apace among citizens in every EU country as they react against further centralisation and control by the EU institutions.

And then we have the drive towards militarisation. In contrast with the establishment parties in the Twenty-Six Counties, Sinn

Féin believes there is no legitimate role for the European Union in military and defence matters, which should be left to individual states. International peacekeeping and conflict resolution should happen under the auspices of the United Nations. In keeping with the commitment to Irish military neutrality, UN primacy, demilitarisation and nuclear disarmament, we believe the Irish government should show leadership and work with others to actively oppose the evolution of an EU Common Defence. Sinn Féin does not support Irish involvement in NATO or any other standing military alliance. The first-hand experience of Irish citizens in the Six Counties is of NATO troops and of how NATO turns a blind eye to the military excesses of one of its member states. We know that our situation has been used as a testing ground of new weapons and surveillance technology, counter-insurgency techniques and crowd-control methods.

We oppose the proposed EU Constitution, which seeks to transform the EU into a global superpower, with its own foreign minister, army and armaments agency. However, for us neutrality does not stop with non-membership of military alliances. It goes further. It means taking fuller responsibility by refusing to facilitate international conflict in any way. It means working for international cooperation and conflict negotiation, democratic social change and respect for human rights. It means working for universal demilitarisation and nuclear disarmament.

A number of years ago, Sinn Féin brought forward a bill to write neutrality into the Irish Constitution for the first time. It was in line with government statements that its policy is opposed to membership of military alliances. Despite this, the government opposed this bill. The reality is that this government is abandoning neutrality by degrees. This is obvious from their policy of allowing US troops to use Shannon on their way to the war in Iraq.

At the Convention on Europe, they didn't even bother to argue for a specific article requiring a UN mandate or an article protecting neutrality. And the so-called "caring coalition" is little better. Fine Gael wants to abandon neutrality and like Labour it is in favour of an EU Common Defence.

The attempt to turn the different member states of Europe

into a single superstate run by a small political, business and bureaucratic elite has gone on for over fifty years, and the certain trend is towards a federal European state. Its gradual stages have been marked by successive treaties, each of which has been presented to the public in the different EU countries as necessary for increasing economic growth and creating jobs. Each, however, has been designed by its advocates to put in place a further element of a highly centralised political system that has many of the features of a supranational EU state.

The first step was the European Coal and Steel Community Treaty in 1950, which put the coal and steel production of France, Germany, Italy and the Benelux countries under a single high authority, the precursor of the EU Commission – "a first step in the federation of Europe". The 1957 Treaty of Rome, which established the European Economic Community (EEC), was the second step. This was a free trade and common market area for manufacturers, with a highly protectionist agricultural policy attached. Thirty years later, in 1987, came the Single European Act, which introduced qualified majority voting on the Council of Ministers for making EU laws that aimed at "harmonising" most policies affecting the internal market and making all forms of national discrimination illegal under European law.

In 1992, the Maastricht Treaty on European Union provided for a single EU currency and a common EU foreign and security policy. In 1998, the Amsterdam Treaty provided for the "progressive framing of a common defence policy". In 2003, the Nice Treaty set out the voting system for a twenty-seven-state EU, and in the following year the EU expanded from fifteen to twenty-five states. In 2004, too, came the "Treaty Establishing a Constitution for Europe", which Belgian Prime Minister Guy Verhofstadt called "the capstone of a European Federal state". This latest EU treaty proposed repealing all the existing EC/EU treaties and founding what would be in effect a new European Union on the basis of its own Constitution, just like any state, rather than on treaties between sovereign states, as hitherto. Article 1.6 of this treaty provides: "The Constitution and law adopted by the institutions of the Union in exercising competences conferred on it shall have primacy over the law of the member states." Article I-12 provides: "The member states shall exercise their competence to the extent that the Union has not exercised or has decided to cease exercising, its competence." Article I-7 proposed to give legal personality to this new Union so that it could sign treaties with other states, something the EU could not previously do. Then Article I-10 provides: "Every national of a member state shall be a citizen of the Union." One can only be a citizen of a state. The EU Constitution, if it should come into force, would therefore make us citizens of this new EU state, with the obligation of obeying that state's laws and giving it our prime allegiance. For the new EU, the Constitution would have supremacy over its member states, and the EU Constitution itself would have legal primacy over the Irish and the other member state's constitutions.

There is much else that is objectionable in the proposed EU Constitution, from the establishment of an EU foreign minister to abolishing the vetoes of member states and giving the EU law-making powers in fifty or so more new policy areas or matters over and above the existing European treaties. In 2005, the revolt of the French and Dutch voters against it has thrown a spanner in the works of the EU state-building project and alerted people everywhere to the threat this poses to their democracy.

I do not believe that the EU can be made more democratic by giving it more powers or proposing Utopian schemes for restructuring the Brussels machinery. In order to increase democracy in the EU, or rather to reduce its lack of democracy, power must be shifted back from Brussels to member states. This point has been conceded by EU elites. The Laeken Declaration which established the Convention from which came the EU Constitution suggested that the Convention should consider the possibility of returning powers from the EU to the member states. Yet the Constitution the Convention produced contained not a single such proposal.

One reform scheme for the EU I am aware of, and which does not call for either its total dissolution or immediate national withdrawal from it, is that put forward by dissenting members of the Convention on the Future of Europe who were opposed to Euro-federalism. This "Alternative Europe of Democracies" was formally presented to the EU Heads of State and Government, and its text was carried in the official report of the Convention to the Intergovernmental Conference (IGC) that finally approved the EU Constitution. This dissenting report proposed, for instance, that EU commissioners should be elected by the parliaments of the EU states and each one should report to his or her parliament regularly. There are other such ideas which would make the EU less undemocratic than it is. Such proposals need to be discussed and lobbied for by EU reformers in the period ahead, as the Euro-federalists regroup after the blow to their EU Constitution project and seek to revive it and push on with further EU integration.

The EU now affects virtually every area of public policy. While I was writing this chapter, the newspapers announced that the latest EU plans would abolish the Irish sugar industry completely and close down the one remaining Carlow sugar factory. The next day they gave details of a row between the VHI and BUPA over how to maintain "community rating" in private health insurance – something that affects over a million people in the Twenty-Six Counties. Community rating is the principle that young and old should pay the same annual health insurance premiums for the same healthcare packages. Before the 1987 Single European Act, the VHI was unique in the world in being a state company with a monopoly in the sale of private health insurance. This kept the costs of administration and health-plan advertising down. Then the EU made such a state monopoly illegal. New companies brought competition, but with it higher administrative and advertising costs, and new difficulties for maintaining community rating and the principle of social solidarity.

Sinn Féin campaigned against membership of the EEC in 1973. Our view was that as a small, partitioned island we would not benefit from what was essentially a rich man's club led in the main by former colonial powers. Since then, each successive European treaty has taken further powers from the Irish state and the other member states and transferred them to Brussels, where the Irish people and the peoples of the other member countries no longer are in control of them. Sinn Féin and Irish republicans have consistently pointed out the fundamentally political and federalist character of the EU project over that time, and its profound lack of democracy.

Our approach to the EU is one of critical engagement: those things that are in the interests of the Irish people, we support and seek to further; those things that are not, we oppose and campaign to change. However, we do not delude ourselves or the Irish people that we can enjoy full democracy or national independence as long as the majority of the laws that now bind us are made by people whom we do not elect and have minimal control over. We want to cooperate with democrats across our continent in building a Europe of equals, where all states, regardless of their size or wealth or power, respect one another's sovereignty and national democracy and cooperate together in tackling the common problems of Europe and the wider world.

We support whatever steps might promote peace, demilitarisation and nuclear disarmament and the just resolution of conflicts under the leadership of a reformed, renewed and more democratic United Nations. We support whatever steps might be taken at EU level to show respect for and promote national, collective and individual rights, and foster economic and social justice in Europe and across the globe. We urge EU support for responsible fair trade policies that help to develop rather than exploit the poor countries of the world. In particular, Sinn Féin campaigns that the EU and its member states commit themselves to the Millennium Development Goals for halving global poverty by 2015. We oppose an EU that aspires to be a political and economic superpower. We oppose further EU centralisation and control, and campaign for the return of EU powers to its member states as the only practical way of reducing its lack of democracy.

We also seek to challenge those in the Irish political establishment who, despite their sham battles, are totally uncritical and shamefully subservient to Brussels in everything that has to do with the EU. Yet the Irish people have very different views, as shown by the rising numbers opposing further EU integration in successive referendum votes in the Twenty-Six Counties. I believe that it is possible to fundamentally change the European Union, to regain the national democracy of member states and to create a Europe of cooperating states. I believe that the crisis caused by the revolt of the peoples of two of the original EEC founders, France and Holland, against an EU constitution could well be the beginning of such an unravelling of Euro-federalism. The powers that be in the EU will naturally fight back, because their careers and political futures are bound up with the integration project. But ordinary people are no longer with them. The peoples of the EU countries are massively disillusioned with the centralised, bureaucratic and undemocratic EU of the elites. For them a better Europe is possible.

Chapter 11

SEIZE THE MOMENT

Writing in 1986 about the IRA and the issue of armed struggle, I commented, "As a means of struggle against the British presence in the Six Counties in pursuance of national independence, armed action represents a necessary form of struggle . . ." In the course of many interviews, speeches and other pronouncements, I had been making the same point for years before this. Defending the right to engage in armed actions and the legitimacy of these actions was a particular consequence of the 1981 hunger strikes and the failed efforts of the British government to criminalise the republican struggle. Of course, any defence of the use of armed struggle was hedged with any number of conditions about how armed actions could be employed, and I for one was always very clear in my mind about this. I was also clear that the term British presence meant the British occupation forces and its infrastructure and administration. I never considered the unionists to be the British presence, and I never glamorised armed actions. It is my very strong view that the deadly business of war and its consequences should never be romanticised.

The main issue was about the question of the legitimacy of armed struggle, and in my view this was clear-cut. In the context of armed occupation, Irish people have the legitimate right to engage in armed resistance. That is a matter of political principle.

Whether this is the correct or appropriate response is another question entirely. That is a matter of tactics. There are also considerable moral problems in relation to armed struggle. I cannot conceive of any thinking person who would not have scruples about inflicting any form of hurt on another living being. It is also my clear and longstanding view that the use of armed struggle was only appropriate in the absence of any alternative means to pursue democratic goals. One of the objectives of Sinn Féin's political work, which culminated in our peace strategy in the 1980s, was the establishment of such an alternative. This is what underpinned my discussions with Fr Alec Reid and Fr Des Wilson from the late 1970s, and the ongoing work through contacts and later discussions with John Hume, the Irish government, Irish America and others in the twenty years or so since then.

The conclusion to all this came on 28 July 2005 when the IRA announced the formal end to its armed campaign. This book need not be concerned with how this was achieved. Suffice to say that there were great difficulties involved. In my view, the potential and the possibilities for progress which have now been created make all this very worthwhile. Aside from all other considerations, the fact is that many hundreds of people who might be dead are spared to live their lives free from the dangers of conflict. Our endeavour has to be to ensure that conflict in Ireland becomes history and that no one else dies or kills because of the political situation in our country.

This places a huge onus on opinion and policy makers in Ireland and abroad, on political parties and leaders and on many other agencies and institutions. It stands to reason that if an alternative way forward through peaceful and democratic means is to succeed, then those in the leadership of our country need to apply themselves to this task. There is also a huge onus on the British government and the international community. But for now I want to concentrate on what the IRA announcement means for republicans and, perhaps more importantly, what does it mean for the republican struggle? What does it mean for the future?

The Irish Republican Army, Óglaigh na hÉireann, takes its historical and organisational origins from the forces which engaged in the Easter Rising of 1916, though its ancestry can be traced much further back. So, too, can the history of armed resistance or physical force republicanism. This goes back over two hundred years to the United Irishmen and the insurrections of 1798. That is the birth of Irish republicanism. Armed actions, resistance and other forms of violent opposition go back beyond that to the first efforts by others to colonise and pacify Ireland by the use of violence. So, for centuries as part of the conquest there have been wars and the threat of wars in Ireland. There have also been other forms of state violence, of coercion and genocide, starvation and dispossession.

This is the historical background to the IRA's recent decision. There is also a personal and contemporary context for many republicans. The decision by the IRA was undoubtedly a deeply emotional one for many. I am sure there will be republicans still trying to come to terms with it many months later. I remember the day after the 1994 IRA cessation was declared, crowds of people visited the Republican Plot in Milltown Cemetery. It was quite spontaneous. My wife Colette bumped into the mother of Mairead Farrell that day. Mairead was killed with two other IRA volunteers in Gibraltar in March 1988. They spoke about the declaration of the cessation. "It was a great day," Mrs Farrell said. "I'm sorry my Mairead wasn't here to see it."

July 28 was another day like that. It will take time for republicans to fully absorb the import of the IRA statement. The decision to move into a new peaceful mode was historic and represented a courageous and confident initiative. It presents an unparalleled challenge and opportunity for every nationalist and republican, placing an enormous responsibility on us to seize the moment and to make Irish freedom a reality.

The IRA initiative also presented challenges to others. While the Irish and the British governments responded warmly to the announcement, and the British government moved speedily on issues like demilitarisation, they still have much to do, particularly on equality and human rights. And, of course, the DUP still stand back from the process. The political institutions established by the Good Friday Agreement remain suspended.

So where stands Irish republicanism today following these unprecedented developments?

Republicans are now in an entirely new area of struggle. There is a role for everyone in this new situation. As this book outlines, republicans have a vision for the future. We want to see an end to British rule in our country. We want to make partition history.

For most of my adult life, the republican struggle has been dominated by the IRA. This is hardly surprising, because for most of that time there has been a war. This war was a consequence of British policy in Ireland, partition and the abandonment by successive Irish governments of people in the north. Efforts by republicans, including myself and Martin McGuinness, to bring it to a negotiated settlement go back over thirty years. Those thirty years have been very difficult ones. Many of us have seen friends, family members, neighbours and comrades die violent deaths. Many republicans have inflicted violent deaths on others. Most of my political peer group have spent long periods incarcerated in British prison camps, prison ships and jails in both parts of Ireland and elsewhere. Some died on hunger strike.

All of that is now behind us. It has shaped us and made us what we are. We will never forget those who have died. How could we? But we have a huge imperative to build a lasting peace and a new political dispensation in our country. Can we do this? I think we can.

When I first joined Sinn Féin towards the end of 1964 and the beginning of 1965, it was a banned organisation. It remained like that for another ten years and even when the ban was removed in the mid-'70s the party was always a very poor second cousin to the IRA. While the ban was never reimposed, censorship was the order of the day in both parts of Ireland. So, efforts to build a political party either fell foul of British or Irish government repression or, more tellingly, self-inflicted theological inertia. All that changed in the wake of the 1981 hunger strikes and the development of the Sinn Féin peace strategy.

Sinn Féin is now the third largest political party on the island and the largest nationalist party in the north. On 6 April 2005, when I appealed to the IRA, I made the point that when there was no alternative I had defended the right of the Army to engage in armed struggle.

"But now," I said, "I believe there is an alternative . . . By building political support for republican and democratic objectives across Ireland and by winning support for these goals internationally." I pointed out that the Ireland we live in today is very different from that of fifteen years ago. "There is an all-Ireland agenda with huge potential. Nationalists and republicans have a confidence that will never again allow anyone to be treated as second-class citizens. Equality is our watchword. The catalyst for much of this change is the growing support for republicanism."

It is my view that this support will continue to grow. The IRA's decision has liberated the situation. Not only can we confidently expect to see the peace process bedded down, but if we all work at it the Good Friday Agreement will be fully implemented. This will not be easy. It will always be a battle a day between those who want maximum change and those who want to maintain the *status quo*. The unionists generally want to do this or at least to delay or dilute the process of change. But they are not on their own. Conservative political parties and others, particularly in the south, are obsessed with stopping Sinn Féin's growing vote. They will not succeed.

When the IRA called off or ended armed campaigns in the past, it was because it faced defeat. Generally speaking, such developments happened because or while republicanism was in the doldrums. That is not the case today. The IRA's initiative was the absolutely right thing for it to do, and that is essentially why it took the decision it did. Because it was the right thing. National liberation struggles can have different phases. There is a time to resist, to stand up and to confront the enemy by arms if necessary. In other words, unfortunately, there is a time for war. There is also a time to engage. To reach out. To put war behind us all. There is a time for peace. There is a time for justice. There is a time for rebuilding. This is that time. That was the essence and the core message of the IRA's announcement.

It is a sign of confidence in the people. Others in the British or unionist armed groups may not have such confidence at this time, but for republicans the way forward has been signposted and the means for advancing our goals have been clearly identified. There will be many problems to be resolved by the people of Ireland in the time ahead.

I believe there now exists for the first time since partition an opportunity for all political parties which espouse Irish unity, and democrats generally who are members of no party, to build a broad movement to debate and plan the type of Ireland we want to live in. A political strategy to deliver unity and independence is required – a strategy which addresses the concerns of unionists but which also carries forward the necessary work of removing partition and the British jurisdiction. In this way we will build the new Ireland and a new national republic in a planned and systematic fashion.

People in struggle are the history makers. As we review and consolidate our position, as we face up to the challenges presented by the peace process, there is a need also to project ourselves ahead ten or twenty years from now. In so doing, we must keep sight of where we want to go and avoid the dangers of being mesmerised by the day-to-day tactical manoeuvres, localised issues and other immediate considerations of the struggle. We are living through a time of great hope, great risk and great opportunity.

GERRY ADAMS
Before the Dawn: An Autobiography

"One thing about him is certain: Gerry Adams is a gifted writer who, if he were not at the center of the war-and-peace business, could easily make a living as an author, of fiction or fact." *New York Times*

ISBN 0 86322 289 7

GERRY ADAMS
Hope and History: Making Peace in Ireland

"A fascinating account of his journey through the peace process, from the first tentative discussions with a priest called Father Reid, to his present position sharing the pages of *Hello*! with The Corrs, the international stage with Nelson Mandela." *Daily Mirror*

ISBN 0 86322 330 3

GERRY ADAMS
An Irish Journal

"Gives an almost personal feel for the peace process as it develops, from Sinn Féin's first meeting with Britain's new prime minister Tony Blair to the build-up to the Good Friday agreement." *Sunday Tribune*

ISBN 0 86322 282 X

GERRY ADAMS
Cage Eleven

"Quite brilliant... a tribute to a particular kind of survival by a group of people who have committed their lives to a deeply held political belief about their country." *Books Ireland*

ISBN 0 86322 292 7

GERRY ADAMS
The Street

"The warmth of Adams's writing comes from the affection of a man for the remembered things of his past... Adams can write well." *Times Literary Supplement*

ISBN 0 86322 293 5

GERRY ADAMS
Selected Writings

"Adams writes fluently and observantly... He displays a hard-edged compassion for the silent poor, the old and the down-and-out." *Financial Times*

ISBN 0 86322 233 1

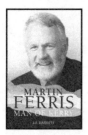

J. J. BARRETT
Martin Ferris: Man of Kerry

"I can recommend this story of how at least one quintessential Kerryman came to beat his sword into a ploughshare. It is a tale told in friendship and admiration by the man best qualified to do it." Tim Pat Coogan

ISBN 0 86322 310 9

TOM REILLY
Joe Stanley: Printer to the Rising

During the Easter Rising of 1916, as the fires burned and the rifles cracked around the GPO, Joe Stanley acted as Pearse's press agent, the leader of the Rising relying on him to get word to the masses that Ireland was rebelling once again.

ISBN 0 86322 346 X

Adrian Hoar
In Green and Red: The Lives of Frank Ryan

"The work is of a high standard, well documented, with index, a list of sources and copious notes... there is hardly a dull moment in the account from beginning to end." *Irish Independent*

ISBN 0 86322 332 X

Sean O'Callaghan
To Hell or Barbados

"An illuminating insight into a neglected episode in Irish history . . . its main achievement is to situate the story of colonialism in Ireland in the much larger context of world-wide European imperialism." *Irish World*

ISBN 0 86322 287 0

Henry Sinnerton
David Ervine: Uncharted Waters

"Revealing . . . Ervine is an impressive advocate of modern unionism." *Irish Examiner*
"[A] valuable contribution to the understanding of the troubles." *Irish World*

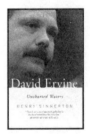

ISBN 0 86322 312 5

Joe Good
Enchanted by Dreams; The Journal of a Revolutionary

A fascinating first-hand account of the 1916 Rising and its aftermath by a Londoner who was a member of the Irish Volunteers who joined the garrison in the GPO.

ISBN 0 86322 225 0

Francis J. Costello
Enduring the Most: The Life and Death of Terence MacSwiney

"Francis J. Costello's comprehensive biography is most welcome... It will surely remain the definitive work."
Sunday Independent

ISBN 0 86322 220 X

Tom Hanahoe
America Rules: US Foreign Policy, Globalization and Corporate USA

The disturbing, definitive account of globalization and the new American imperialism.

ISBN 0 86322 309 5

Frank Connolly (ED)
The Christy Moore Songbook

Over a hundred songs, with music, illustrated with photos. "Christy Moore is the most successful solo artist in Ireland." *In Dublin*

ISBN 0 86322 063 0

Gerard Ronan
The Irish Zorro

"Comprehensive and enthralling . . . truly extraordinary... Ronan's passion and sympathy for his subject shine through so it reads like a novel. A 'must read'."
Irish Independent

ISBN 0 86322 329 X